The State We're In

Praise for *The 2009 Flux Trend Review*

'*Flux Trend Review* has become my marketing bible. It has helped me to understand the South African youth culture and to strategise for events like Youth Day. PESTLE analysis has never been this zhoozh. So insightful and current that almost every page has an idea. I think every marketer should own a copy.'
Thulani Mahlangu, Brand Assistant: In-Restaurant Experience, Nando's National Marketing

'Most trend forecasts available are based on what's happening outside our country and continent. Dion Chang's *Flux Trend Review* is a unique and much-needed resource of what's going on in SA.'
Kassie Naidoo, Creative Director, King James Group

'In my position time for reading is scarce – but it is also essential to stay up to date with the latest research, competitor and market activities and trends. The format of the *Flux Trend Review* really made life easier, as it meant I could easily fit in a chapter in between other essential reading ... And it gave me new insights into areas where my finger is not so close to the pulse – but perhaps should have been.'
Jacqui McKeown, Head: Sanlam Market Intelligence, Sanlam Group Marketing

'The *Flux Trend Review* was a timely and concise intervention in our irreversible reality of information overload. It was as useful for professionals in the various creative and media industries as the curious observer on the periphery.'
Siphiwe Mpye, Associate Editor GQ (South Africa)

'A unique futuristic publication that is informative and insightful in all realms of the business and creative worlds. *Flux Trend Review* is a supportive reference used frequently by Financial Junction Investments in its management of and wealth creation for its clients.'
Lynn Marais, Financial Junction Investments (Pty) Ltd

The State We're In
The 2010 Flux Trend Review

Edited by Dion Chang

MACMILLAN

First published 2009
by Pan Macmillan South Africa
Private Bag X19
Northlands
Johannesburg
2116

www.panmacmillan.co.za
www.fluxtrends.co.za

ISBN 978-1-77010-166-1

Editing by Laurice Taitz
Proofreading by Andrea Nattrass
Design and typesetting by Triple M Design, Johannesburg
Cover design and chapter symbols by Nicework Communications

Printed and bound by Ultra Litho (Pty) Limited

Contents

LIFESTYLE REVIEW

About Flux Trends

WE ARE discovering that life in the 21st century is nothing we imagined it would be. We find ourselves bombarded with information 24 hours a day, 7 days a week, 365 days a year. The onslaught is relentless. We have less time to absorb, less time to reflect and, as a result, less time to make measured or informed decisions.

As a matter of survival, not choice, we edit the information flung at us and discard what is not within our immediate area of interest. The only problem is that the information we edit out (and don't believe is relevant) is becoming increasingly interconnected so we inadvertently block or divert our information channels. As a result, our perspective is skewed, our social interaction is affected, the generation gap becomes wider and we start to miss out on crucial business opportunities.

Too much information is becoming counterproductive.

The Flux Trend Review is literally an opportunity to hit the 'pause' button. The Flux byline is: 'The State We're In' and the Flux Trend Review aims to provide you with a snapshot of 'the state we're in' across a number of industries that have a direct influence on our daily lives, the way we interact with each other, and ultimately, the way we do business with each other.

The annual Flux Trend Review is now in its third year. The concept began as a trend conference and morphed into book format last year. It has a growing following and is used as an essential business and reference tool by a cross-section of industries, from marketing departments and corporate executives, to journalists and students.

Its holistic approach provides insights into global trends, but also offers a South African perspective of those trends.

In this 2010 edition we track the ripple effect of the global economic meltdown, the consumer revolution that has been sparked off as a result, the technology that has provided the tools for change, and the massive shift of social and business dynamics that are altering the journey ahead.

The 2010 Flux Trend Review may cover some trends that are already bubbling to the surface, and some trends you might never have heard about or considered important. But beyond that, what it does is join the dots and show the impact that these trends have on one another, and how that is changing our lives.

In a nutshell, the Flux Trend Review is a social commentary service that identifies lifestyle trends that affect the way in which we live, work and do business in the 21st century.

Aren't you curious to discover what state we're in?

Acknowledgements

GATHERING INFORMATION and researching trends for this book is no easy task. As technology increases the pace of the world, tracking the full impact of an emerging trend is like trying to catch a slippery eel with your bare hands.

Fortunately, I have a dedicated team of trend spotters who are passionate about fishing in a sea of change – while a storm is raging. They cast their nets far and wide and not only bring back new ideas and unusual insights but also join the dots and make unexpected connections that only with hindsight seem obvious.

Heartfelt thanks to Loren Phillips and Sarah Badat – the core team at Flux – for their hard work and unique take on the world, and to Carina Louw, a trend observer of note, and also Milisuthando Bongela and Sandiso Ngubane for their contributions.

To this year's specialist contributors: my thanks and appreciation for sharing your wisdom and insights. It is through your eyes that we are able to see past the smoke and mirrors and discern what's really important, and what we should be focusing on.

To the team at Pan Macmillan: thank you for having faith in the Flux Trend Review concept and providing the 2009 edition with such an incredible launch pad, as well as a vote of confidence for the 2010 edition.

To my editor Laurice Taitz, my respect and gratitude. Pulling to-gether a trend anthology like this must be like working the switch-board at the United Nations.

Finally to my partner, Chris, and my mom, Jenny: thanks for

keeping the home fires burning … and the freezer stocked. No one truly understands or appreciates the joys of individually packaged, home-cooked meals until they try to put together a book.

Introduction

Nursing a global hangover

Dion Chang

Dion Chang is an innovator, creative thinker and visionary. He is a sought-after trend analyst, and while his feet remain firmly planted on African soil, he uses a global perspective to source new ideas, gauge the zeitgeist and identify cutting-edge trends. Local and international corporations have turned to him as a consultant, because of his ability to think outside the box. For fifteen years he has worked in various fields in the magazine and fashion industries, and currently operates as a trend analyst, freelance journalist and columnist, specialising in social commentary. He has written a book based on his popular cartoon character, Gloria, has sat on the judging panel of South Africa's premier magazine awards, and has faced the nation as a TV presenter.

IN *The 2009 Flux Trend Review* I referred to 2008 as 'the year of the wake-up call', and what a wake-up call it has been. Globally we have all experienced a rather rude awakening and it seems that we spent the first half of 2009 nursing a bruising hangover from the boom-time party we had thought would never end. That party is well and truly over, and we have been tasked with cleaning up the messy aftermath, and in the process, rearranging the odd bits of furniture that were toppled while it was in full swing.

The process of rearranging our furniture – and therefore the way in which we live – is proving to be surprisingly cathartic. Admittedly, the blurred vision and depression that accompany such hangovers have not been pleasant. They have, however, made us vow (as one does when in recovery mode) not to repeat such excesses ever again. Will we stick to that pledge?

Only time will tell. But for now the sentiment does seem sincere. Perhaps it is slowly dawning on us that there is too much at stake for any recalcitrant behaviour.

The tide is turning

Globally, the promise to change our ways has been evident. A sense of determination to do things differently and not repeat mistakes of the past has reverberated around the world. One of the most notable shifts in mindset has been the new Barack Obama administration in the USA. Obama's election has been a benchmark of change, not only in the USA but also for the rest of the world. The stark contrast between the Bush and Obama administrations illustrates what so many trend spotters, futurists and scenario planners have been predicting: that we are witnessing a universal shift in attitude and thinking – from a greedy and power-hungry society to one that is more ethically based.

The expense claims scandal in British politics, which outraged the tax-paying public and resulted in many cabinet ministers falling on their swords demonstrates this new mood perfectly. Similarly, the outrage in America that erupted after AIG executives awarded themselves bonuses using the government's bailout package points to a civil society that is no longer willing to put up with, or place its trust in, governments that are not accountable or big businesses that are not transparent.

In essence, the global economic meltdown has served as the instrument that has lanced the boil of greed, corruption, mismanagement and deceit. It has left many around the world poorer, but infinitely wiser. Ironically, the trail of devastation that the global recession has left in its wake has cleared the way for new ideas, new beginnings and, most importantly, new value systems.

Caring and sharing – all together now

While there has been a growing realisation that the eco movement is not so much someone else's problem but an individual's responsibility, the global recession has amplified this new-found mood of mindfulness.

As retrenchments increased, the global sensitivity gauge

seemed to rise accordingly. Collaboration, cooperation, caring and sharing became the buzzwords for a wounded society. Job sharing and corporate collaboration became the new, and accepted, means of survival. Recycling and reusing – activities previously associated solely with the eco movement – suddenly became benchmarks of good business practice and the core philosophy of all lifestyle trends: from fashion to interiors. Even cookbooks reflected this new austerity.

The importance of having a wide and dependable social network has never been more evident. It was the way in which many survived the recession: finding leads for rare job interviews, or simply pooling resources when times got really tough. It is ironic that when this need was most pronounced technology provided the perfect tools. Is it sheer coincidence that social networks like Facebook and Twitter came into their own when people needed them most, or did these networks boom because of people's needs? Either way, they have forever changed the way in which we communicate, socialise and do business. They may seem like time-wasting frivolities to many, but their long-term impact and effect on human interaction and social dynamics have yet to be fully revealed.

Don't look back, can't look back

There are key industries that have already reached life-changing crossroads. The print media industry is struggling to survive, or at the very least reinvent itself – fast. As Jeff Bezos (Amazon's CEO and the brain behind the Kindle DX e-reader) remarked in an interview with *Fortune* magazine: 'I don't want to oversimplify what's happening in the media ... But I find it hard to believe that the primary way of reading newspapers ten-plus years from now is going to be on printed paper.'[1] Makes you stop and think, doesn't it?

Glossy magazines will be next in the firing line and that industry is already scrabbling to find ways to reinvent itself. It may take a while for it to arrive at that crossroads, but the warning signs are there.

Similarly, the advertising industry is faced with a massive rethink of how it speaks to, and reaches, consumers who are becoming more and more difficult to define and segment using the traditional methods of profiling that are fast becoming obsolete. New technologies are providing new avenues, new tools and therefore, new experiences for consumers, who are tired of being talked at, and prefer to be engaged in a two-way conversation. As this year's social media expert, Mike Stopforth, quotes in his chapter: 'A powerful global conversation has begun. Through the Internet people are discovering and inventing new ways to share relevant knowledge with blinding speed. As a direct result markets are getting smarter – and getting smarter faster than most companies.'

The days of marketing to, or being able to reach, the largest numbers of people are long gone. The online world has provided a sense of freedom and empowerment that the offline world is struggling to match: we call it *the change gap*, and it gets wider every day.

However, within that gap something special is happening. The faceless masses are banding together in clusters – what all marketing people now refer to as 'tribes'. These tribes have formed and converged on the basis of shared interests and thanks to the Internet there are no boundaries. Geography, race and cultural differences dissolve in cyberspace, and all that matters are shared interests and connectivity with like-minded friends. In the words of marketing guru, Seth Godin (who coined the term 'tribes'): '[If you want to] you can even find Ukrainian folk dancers, and connect with them, because you want to be connected.'[2]

The significance of this urge to be connected cannot be underestimated. When coupled with the mood of uncertainty that is sweeping across the planet, it becomes the glue that bonds communities and tribes closer together. It comes as no surprise, then, that old-fashioned word-of-mouth referral has become the backbone of this new society. Young girls, for example, are said to be more trusting of their peers when it comes to fashion advice than of a glossy magazine's fashion editor. Similarly, the distrust towards banks and financial institutions as a result of the economic meltdown has also resulted in people preferring referrals from friends or trusted sources.

We are witnessing the emergence and convergence of new communities, brought together by new rules and ever-evolving needs. These communities, or tribes, are rising up and changing the world on their terms, and their choice of weapon is technology.

The tribes have spoken.

There is no looking back – but then again, why would you?

Notes

1 Jeff Bezos in Jeffrey O'Brien, 'Amazon's Next Revolution'. CNN Money.com, 26 May 2009, www. money.cnn.com/2009/05/26/technology/obrien_kindle.fortune/index.htm?section=money_latest (accessed 4 August 2009).
2 Seth Godin, 'Seth Godin on the Tribes we Lead'. TED Talk, February 2009, www.ted.com/talks/seth_godin_on_the_tribes_we_lead.html (accessed 4 August 2009).

Pulse of the people

Is our miracle rainbow nation turning out to be just another country?

Mondli Makhanya

Mondli Makhanya is the Editor-in-Chief of *The Sunday Times*, the most-read weekly newspaper in South Africa. He is a regular commentator on current affairs and also sits on the council of the South African National Editors' Forum. Makhanya previously served as Editor of the *Mail & Guardian* and as both Deputy Managing Editor and Political Editor of *The Sunday Times*. He has worked in a variety of journalistic capacities on a range of newspapers including the *Weekly Mail*, *The Star* and *Sunday World*. Makhanya is married and lives in Johannesburg.

THE STORY goes that soon after a top Johannesburg advertising agency received a prestigious award at the Cannes Lions International Advertising Festival, a young black creative at the company posted a comment on the Bizcommunity website bemoaning the state of affairs and lack of transformation at the company. The big shots at the agency mounted a witch-hunt that resulted in them outing the employee.

The scene was set for a cross-generational, racial conflict. The Managing Director of the company, a middle-aged white male, was fuming. How dare she be this disloyal?

The young woman, in her early twenties, was initially defiant, believing that it was her democratic right to voice her opinions on the goings on at her workplace. It was time to talk truth to white power she felt. In the end, though, she relented. She apologised and was sanctioned by her employers but the air was poisoned and a settlement was reached, in terms of which she left the company.

This clash represents the undercurrents in South African society: white power versus frustrated black ambition.

There is another story that may sound very much like urban legend but is about an actual incident that took place some years ago, long before xenophobic violence exploded across the country.

A foreign national was using a public phone and as this was an occasional long-distance call to the family back home he was on the line for a long time. A queue built up until impatience got the better of those behind him. They yanked the receiver from his hand and manhandled him.

'First you took our jobs and then you took our women. Now you are taking our telephones too,' the man relayed the sentiments of his harassers to a national radio station.

There's more. In the run up to the ANC's Limpopo conference in 2008 a pamphlet circulated among the party's structures calling for Tsonga (Shangaan) speakers to ensure the displacement of 'inferior' ethnic groups and for the election of one of their own to the chairmanship and ultimately the premiership of the province:

> The Great King Soshangane was not leading a tribe but a nation. Throughout history our nation has been looked down upon by mere tribes. An example is the Lobedu clan, which up to today does not allow our subjects to enter their 'royal' house. Another example is the Pedi tribe, which all along has been referring derogatorily to our subjects as makwapa [subhuman]. The time for redress is now.[1]

'For the coming provincial conference we have tried and tested patriotic sons of Soshangane who have demonstrated their unflinching commitment to the empowerment of our great nation,' the anonymously penned pamphlet urged.

Or consider this story: in the aftermath of the ANC's victory and the inauguration of President Jacob Zuma, he appointed a cabinet broadly representative of South Africa's demographics. At least so he believed.

But away from his Union Buildings office there were grumblings from senior leadership and ordinary members because he had given all the economic ministries to white, coloured and Indian ministers. 'Does this mean Africans cannot count?' was the sentiment expressed in many quarters.

It is the sort of stuff we do not talk about much, these undercurrents of our existence.

We smile, we laugh, we converse and we celebrate our supposed Rainbow Nation status, but beneath the surface we remain a divided people. So have we been deluding ourselves by calling this the Rainbow Nation? Has it all been a mirage, a figment of the imagination of an iconic archbishop or the unrealised ambition of an even more iconic statesman? Have we stood still or gone backwards since May 1994, when in his inauguration speech Nelson Mandela said:

> We have triumphed in the effort to implant hope in the breasts of the millions of our people. We enter into a covenant that we shall build the society in which all South Africans, both black and white, will be able to walk tall, without any fear in their hearts, assured of their inalienable right to human dignity – a rainbow nation at peace with itself and the world.[2]

Was Archbishop Desmond Tutu too ambitious when he declared in the early days of our democracy that we were 'the rainbow people of God'? Or was Thabo Mbeki just dreaming when he gave his 'I am an African' speech on the day of the adoption of the nation's founding document and said: 'The Constitution whose adoption we celebrate constitutes an unequivocal statement that we refuse to accept that our Africanness shall be defined by our race, colour, and gender of historical origins. It is a firm assertion made by ourselves that South Africa belongs to all who live in it, black and white.'[3]

The simple answer to this is that we did little to match vision with application. The transition from a divided and oppressive apartheid South Africa to an equitable non-racial democratic one was always going to be rocky. It was never going be about waving a magic wand and making it happen.

Firstly, there were going to be issues of redress, which inevitably would cause distress to the previously privileged. Enter the policies of affirmative action, or employment equity, as the new administration called it. Given the experience of other countries that had implemented this redress mechanism, it was inevitable that there was going to be resistance. Reversing the effects of a system that had been based on white superiority and black exclusion needed to take some form of social engineering. So legislation was enacted compelling corporates to set targets for the transformation of their workplaces. These targets, which were later spelt out in regulatory codes involved quotas on the employment of black people, women and disabled people.

Predictably this resulted in major resentment from the white population that was already reeling from a sense of loss of power in society. The wave of resentment swept through white South Africa and many – young and old – felt that they were no longer wanted and should rather seek greener pastures abroad.

There were lots of myths around affirmative action fuelled by political parties and narrow interest groups. Though not backed up by any empirical evidence, white society thought reverse apartheid would now be applied and all jobs would be reserved for blacks.

The truth, however, is that more than a decade since the inception of affirmative action corporate power remains in white hands and many black employees still feel very much on the outside and resentful of the whites that still run the corporations. Cue the young woman at the advertising agency.

The affirmative-action-phobic sentiments were not only confined to the white community but also to the coloured and Indian communities who – even though they were classified black in terms of the legislation – felt they were going to be victims rather than beneficiaries of this policy.

Instead of merely effecting necessary redress, the policy seemed to have the effect of dividing South Africa further.

Then Transnet Managing Director and erstwhile ANC heavyweight Saki Macozoma mulled over this question in his farewell speech to the organisation in 2000. He said he had been grappling with the question of how, in the context of implementing demographic change in Transnet, he could inspire young white graduates to believe that they had a future and that it was possible for them to rise to his position.

Affirmative action's twin sister, black economic empowerment, would have the same effect. Intended as a means of giving previously excluded groups a stake in the economy it was to be interpreted by white South Africans as a means of edging them out. Again, with no empirical evidence, the policy was labelled reverse racism.

Blacks, by contrast, believed it was being implemented too slowly and railed against the intransigence of white business on this score.

There were indeed many problems with both 'affirmative action' and 'empowerment' – mostly related to cronyism and greed – but the philosophical basis for their institution was sound.

In the end it was all about political management. All these changes were happening at a time when South Africa's political parties were finding their ideological space in a new society and grappling with what it meant to be a political formation in a free country. Political parties as anywhere in the world will find ways to exploit the fears, hopes and wants of their constituents. So the ANC played to the desires of the black majority who wanted edible fruits of their freedom. The Democratic Party/Alliance played to the concerns of white South Africa (and to a certain extent other minorities), who feared that they were to become the new oppressed, the new excluded.

In this macabre dance were two main players: Thabo Mbeki and Tony Leon. While Mbeki saw himself as leader of the black majority rather than all the people of South Africa, Leon shrank his role to being the defender of minority interests. In doing so the two men re-divided the country and stalled our journey to a non-racial country.

You only need to listen to radio talk shows and read the letters to the editor to get the feel of just how all our issues are racialised: crime, corruption, international relations, service delivery, sporting triumphs and disappointments. There's a whole racial blame game and a racial defensiveness that themes our discourse. Voting patterns in elections remain racially entrenched, with issues taking the back seat.

Because we have talked ourselves into our corners and enclaves, we really have not had the conversation about what it is to be a South African; about what defines us as a people beyond the fact that we share the same geographic space. What are the commonalities between the Xhosa-speaking person in Mthatha and the Venda-speaking person in Vhembe? Between the Afrikaans-speaking coloured person in Paarl and the English-speaking person in Howick? Between the Indian resident of Laudium and the person of Portuguese origin in Johannesburg's southern suburbs?

What do the middle-class yuppies in the pubs and on the golf courses of our metropolitan suburbs have in common beyond their common interest in single malt whiskey and Tiger Woods?

And, in defining South Africanness, have we accepted that it is not only those of us who were here before Nelson Mandela's release who are South African? Have we accepted that since that February day in 1990 the number of tongues and dialects spoken in our land has probably jumped from about 20 to well over 100? That these immigrants – be they Bangladeshi, Somali, Russian, Zimbabwean or Costa Rican – are all here to stay?

It would appear not, judging by the manner in which we deal with them in officialdom and in our daily interactions. We still see them as people in transit who should be despised, denied rights and occasionally beaten to a pulp or set alight. The sooner we get over this the better.

Today's South Africa is much more of a rainbow than the one

Tutu painted in 1994. We just haven't gotten round to embracing all the colours.

Having painted a rather bleak picture of just how far we have not progressed, it is necessary to point out that few societies compress such dramatic change into so short a space. It is good to be hard on ourselves but we must remember that it was only fifteen years ago that we dumped one of the most evil systems devised by man and decided to become an ideal society.

In this, there are things to be celebrated and built upon. Reasons for hope.

The first is the integration among the younger people in the middle class. Some may say, correctly, that this is a small pool considering that the majority of South Africans are working class and poor. Nonetheless it is a start, and as the middle class burgeons non-racialism may find its defining space in this generation, which will be leading our society in the next few decades.

The only caution here is that this integration should not merely represent the assimilation of black youth culture by a dominant white culture, as evidenced by the rejection of their mother tongue in favour of English by many in this stratum.

The other positive of this is that interests are coalescing, albeit often still a one-way street. Witness the interest in the townships in the fortunes of the Proteas, the Springboks and Super 14 teams. Music, too, is beginning to find a crossover appeal – Mandoza's famed 'Nkalakatha' hit being a case in point.

You are seeing it in the readership of mainstream newspapers where South Africans get a chance to peek into each other's spaces. It is there on radio drive-time shows where celebrity DJs are shared across racial divides.

These examples may seem inane or 'soft' but they can nonetheless be areas where South Africans can find themselves beyond the politics. It may well then be that the politicians will someday have to follow ordinary South Africans to this centre space because they themselves will have been left behind on the extremes.

But this should not preclude the leadership – both political and economic – from starting to chart the path we lost in the past decade or so. The current mood of change and anticipation provides the right climate for the examination of the issues outlined above. The Zuma era – with all its complications – has opened up space for frank and open discussion.

The Americans have a great way of returning to the collective wisdom of their founding fathers and successive generations whenever they are confronted with directional conundrums. They are not shy to flip the pages back and ask: what would so and so have done, and what did they mean when they said A, B, C or D?

Without being overly sentimental, we should be able to revisit our founding fathers and mothers and ask them what they had in mind when they set us on our path.

It is a question best answered by Macozoma in a speech on the preservation of the Mandela legacy that he gave in Zurich in late 2008. There he argued that when talking about the Mandela legacy some 'put emphasis on reconciliation to the exclusion of everything else' while 'some choose to put emphasis on elements that have the potential to advance their interests, ideological and material'.[4]

He argued that we should see Mandela's legacy in its totality: reversing the vagaries of apartheid racism while at the same time 'fostering national integration':

> *Mandela promoted sensitivity to the issue of cultural and political minorities on the part of the African majority. He wanted to ensure that the diversity, which is the strength of our society, is respected and promoted. By teaching and*

by precept Mandela promoted the idea that the individual must relegate the self, self-interest and group interest and subordinate those to the interests of the rainbow nation. What matters, he emphasised, is the people and their agenda rather than the individual leader and his interests.[5]

This can and should be achieved through honest dialogue. It is open dialogue that will bridge the chasm between the likes of the young woman and her boss at the advertising agency, between the racial and ethnic poles of our society.

Through these conversations we will come to a determination of what it is to be a South African.

Notes

1 ANC pamphlet distributed at the 52nd National Congress of the ANC in Justice Malala, 'ANC Descends into Tribalism'. The Times Online, 28 July 2008, www.thetimes.co.za/Columnists/Article.aspx?id=810069 (accessed 29 June 2009).

2 Nelson Rolihlahla Mandela, 'Statement of the President of the African National Congress at his Inauguration as President of the Democratic Republic of South Africa'. ANC, 10 May 1994, www.anc.org.za/ancdocs/speeches/inaugpta.html (accessed 29 June 2009).

3 Thabo Mbeki, 'Statement of Deputy President TM Mbeki on Behalf of the African National Congress on the Occasion of the Adoption by the Constitutional Assembly of the Republic of South Africa Constitution Bill 1996'. ANC, 8 May 1996, www.anc.org.za/ancdocs/history/mbeki/1996/sp960508.html (accessed 29 June 2009).

4 Saki Macozoma, 'Unsurpassed and Indestructible'. *The Times*, 9 November 2008, www.thetimes.co.za/PrintEdition/Insight/Article.aspx?id=880456 (accessed 29 June 2009).

5 Macozoma, 'Unsurpassed and Indestructible'.

Business in Africa

Is Africa the final business frontier?

Rutger-Jan van Spaandonk

Rutger-Jan (RJ) van Spaandonk has been described by *The Sunday Times* as 'a Dutch professional entrepreneur whose pet challenge since 1998 has been to make African businesses profitable', and as 'Nintendo's larger-than-life representative in South Africa'. Since co-founding the Mitchell Madison Group office in Johannesburg, Van Spaandonk has worked in Africa for more than eleven years, representing a variety of companies across industries and working for both public and private-sector organisations predominantly in West, East and Southern Africa. He is currently the Executive Director in charge of strategy and new business development at Core Group, representing some of the world's premier personal technology brands, including Apple and Nintendo. Van Spaandonk is also the founder and Managing Director of Rand Carlton Partners, a Johannesburg-based investment and advisory firm specialising in market entry, venture development and business expansion in frontier markets. He recently turned his widely acclaimed '49 Bullets for Killer Presentations' training into an executive academy for public speaking and presentations, running corporate and individual training programmes. Finally, as the Epicurean Sybarite he comments on luxury lifestyle matters, contributing to a number of publications, including *Wanted* and *GQ*. Van Spaandonk holds a Master's degree in Business Administration (MBA) from the Wharton School of the University of Pennsylvania (USA) and a Bachelor of Business Administration (BBA) from Nijenrode University (Netherlands).

PETER SCHWARTZ, a distinguished futurologist and Chairman of the Global Business Network, wrote an alarming column that appeared in *Red Herring* in November 2000. Not many people took notice of or offence from his article 'The African Time Machine' but it made an indelible impression on me, given that I had recently started considering broadening my activities into the rest of Africa. Schwartz started by saying:

> *Africa is like a vast time machine slowly retreating back into the 19th century. From the Sahara to the South African border most of the countries on the continent are losing ground. Most are poorer today than a decade ago. Violence is endemic. Many have less infrastructure today than 20 years ago. And, of course, AIDS is ravaging the population.*[1]

After highlighting the various ills of Africa and their root causes, he asserted:

> *There is no good scenario for Africa in the next several decades. Perhaps the best case is a slow decline and gradual recovery ... Far more likely is a massive catastrophe and the response to it. Devastation on a scale difficult to imagine is gradually unfolding, driven in part by the AIDS epidemic.*[2]

He then concluded that the 'response [of the international community] to this immense tragedy is likely to be mainly nothing. There will be many international conferences held and even some promises made. But there will be little action and even less fulfilment of promises.'[3]

Seven fat years

Fast forward to the third quarter of 2007 when the recent global financial crisis announced itself by way of a sudden drop in the value of derivatives, particularly ones linked to the residential mortgage market in the USA. I had just finished the pitch book for an African private equity fund that I was attempting to launch, and in which I had concluded:

> *Africa has become an interesting destination for private equity investment. After years of being perceived as the 'dark continent' eternally besieged by war and famine, Africa is now appearing on the radar screen of both financial and strategic investors because of the high economic growth rates and relative socio-economic stability of the key regions.*[4]

Since 2001, Gross Domestic Product (GDP) growth in Africa has been higher than in the rest of the world, and oil-exporting and politically stable countries in particular have been growing more than 5% per annum in real terms for over a decade.

It is clear that Africa had entered an era of structural recovery at the beginning of this century. A new generation of leadership emerged with a global mindset and a free-market perspective. Away from the international limelight these new leaders started improving national and corporate governance. Fiscal discipline was imposed on national, regional and local governments. Key economic sectors were liberalised, state-owned enterprises privatised, and pension and other financial reforms enacted. The terms of trade had improved – with the demand from China, India and Russia for natural resources fuelling a boom in commodities. And many well-trained and experienced Africans were keen to return from Europe and the USA to pursue business and entrepreneurial opportunities in Africa.

So, in a relatively short period of less than seven years the outlook for Africa drastically changed. Mr Schwartz seems to have been spectacularly wrong. Africa had come out of the doldrums, and the private sector was paying attention, born witness to by the interest of hedge fund and private equity investors, and the increased levels of Foreign Direct Investment (FDI).

He was correct about one thing, though. The international community made lots of promises and broke most of them, with the 2005 G8 Summit at Gleneagles[5] serving as a prime, but sad example.

Seven lean years?

Fast forward to the start of 2009; the global financial crisis is out of control, and the economic downturn is the worst since The Great Depression of the 1930s.

Since African banks were hardly exposed to the toxic assets that were bringing banks in Europe and the USA down, it took longer for the recession to hit the continent's shores. But hit it eventually did.

Commodity prices have come down, and so has international demand for them, hurting Africa's export revenues. Official Development Assistance (ODA) is expected to drop now that donor countries have to tighten their belts. FDI is also expected to plummet as a result of the credit crisis. And the African diaspora, suffering from the economic downturn, has cut remittances.

Tourism to and within Africa has abated. Trade finance is difficult to obtain, hindering import and export transactions. Bond markets are closing down for all but the most creditworthy of companies.

The African Development Bank expects exports across Africa to drop by 40% in 2009 and average GDP growth to slow to 2.8%, which is below the rate of population growth[6] (but still much higher than the developed economies that are almost all expected to shrink).

But these statistics belie the vast opportunities that Africa offers. Structurally, nothing has changed since 2008 and all the positive drivers are still in place – only the momentum is gone. It is for this reason that the continent's leaders decry the rich countries for making Africans suffer from a crisis that is not of their own making.

A good indicator of the potential is the fact that South Africa's exports to the rest of Africa for the first quarter of 2009 were up by 35% compared to the first quarter of 2008.[7] For the twelve months ending April 2009, exports were 45% higher than the same period for the previous year.

So, can we affirmatively answer the question: 'Is Africa the next and final frontier for business?'

Africa's potential

Benjamin Zander, the famous conductor of the Boston Philharmonic, told his audience at a leadership talk for TED[8] in 2008:

> Probably a lot of you know the story of the two salesmen who went down to Africa in the 1900s. They were sent down to find if there was any opportunity for selling shoes. And they wrote telegrams back to Manchester. And one of them wrote: 'Situation hopeless. Stop. They don't wear shoes.' And the other one wrote: 'Glorious opportunity. They don't have any shoes yet.'[9]

More than a hundred years later the world can still be divided into a large camp of pessimists that see no future for Africa and a smaller band of entrepreneurs that see vast opportunities. Luckily, the optimists are gaining ground.

From a purely economic point of view, Africa is a lot bigger and richer than many may think, especially when comparing the continent and its individual countries to the fashionable emerging BRIC countries (Brazil, Russia, India and China).[10]

According to the most recent World Bank data for 2008,[11] Africa as a continent has 980 million inhabitants, and a GDP of just over US$1.5 trillion. This compares favourably with, for example, Brazil (US$1.6 trillion), India (US$1.2 trillion) and Russia (US$1.6 trillion). Granted, they are countries, but very large ones – not unlike small continents – with regional differences, logistical challenges and decentralised governmental authorities. If they are big enough to be attractive as markets and investment destinations, why can't Africa?

Looking at the data more critically, we can draw even more interesting conclusions. Assuming that national income data, and especially per capita figures, are a true reflection of the market potential of the BRICs, we find that twelve countries in Africa have a higher Gross National Income (GNI) per capita than China (and 21 African countries higher than India), with a combined population of close to 125 million people (over 450 million people when compared to India). And the whole of Africa has a per capita GNI that is slightly higher than India's. From this angle, Africa looks attractive.

What's more, the Pareto Principle (or 80/20 rule) strictly applies. The ten top economies in Africa (just shy of 20% of the countries) generate around 79% of the continent's wealth, housing almost 47% of the African population. As for potential: although around 15% of the world's population lives in Africa, Africans only produce around 2.6% of global GDP. Very simply put, Africa has to grow by five or six times just to *catch up* with the rest of the world.[12]

Challenges or opportunities?

A lot has been said and written about Africa in relation to corruption, aid dependency, lacklustre governance, failing infrastructure, lack of proper legal frameworks, the dearth of capital and brain drain. I agree that these are all real and an impediment to growth but while Western countries are berating African governments, Asian countries (with China as the flag bearer of the movement) are already building infrastructure, setting up subsidiaries and selling their products in African markets. We can question their motives and practices, as many do, but they are capitalising on the potential that Africa has to offer.

Remember how Asian countries used to attract similarly negative views? In his 1990 seminal *Harvard Business Review* article 'The Competitive Advantage of Nations' Michael Porter, a leading authority on competitive strategy, said India was not an attractive industrial model in spite of its 'low wages and low labour costs'.[13] After India's then Finance Minister (and current Prime Minister) Dr Manmohan Singh started a programme of drastic economic reform the country became the leading centre for outsourced back-office services; one of its sons got to be the world's number one steel magnate within two decades, and Tata bagged the venerable Land Rover and Jaguar automotive brands. I don't see why similar positive developments could not take shape in Africa.

So, where others see challenges, I see opportunities. If it was easy doing business in Africa, every company would be here, and the ability to generate above-average rates of return would no longer exist, making it a less attractive market for early movers and real entrepreneurs.

Generic opportunities in Africa

In modern history – during colonial times and after liberation – most nations and businesses have treated Africa merely as a place from which to extract natural resources ranging from oil and gas to minerals and timber. But in order to harness the full potential we need to start to see Africa as:

1. *A consumer market* – for imported and locally produced products;
2. *An incubator* – for new products, services and business models; and
3. *An exporter* – for agricultural products and talent, among other things.

It goes beyond the scope of this piece to cover these areas in detail, but let's look at some concrete examples of opportunities in each category.

Africa as a consumer market

Most international (luxury) brands already service the elite in many African countries; it is very easy to find a BMW or a bottle of Dom Pérignon in almost any African capital. But more and more, foreign companies are offering their products and services to the emerging middle class. With rising income levels come economic aspirations, ultimately growing the consumer market potential in each country. Often companies don't have to change the product or price (as measured by volumes) as long as one factors in the lack of large-scale retail and quantities of serving (single servings versus family-size packaging).

An interesting case is that of PZ Cussons of the UK that offers its brands of personal care, home care and nutrition products in established markets (UK and Australia), emerging markets (Indonesia and Poland) and frontier markets (Nigeria, Ghana and Kenya). Although the company originated out of a trading business in West Africa, it exemplifies how a portfolio of similar consumer products might be leveraged throughout the world in markets at different stages of development, simply by localising brands and production and distribution models. As a result, an ever-growing portion of its global turnover emanates from Africa (47% in 2008 versus 40% in 2006).[14]

Equally telling in this light is the growth of South African retail concepts throughout Africa, especially from PEP Stores, Shoprite and Woolworths, with 300, 70 and 31 stores respectively in African countries outside of South Africa.[15]

The next step in market penetration is to develop products for the bottom end of the market. For example, Safaricom of Kenya and Vodafone of the UK developed a service called M-PESA which allows customers to transfer money using a mobile phone, even if they don't have a bank account. The service has been so successful that it is now being rolled out into other frontier countries.

Africa as an incubator

In 1935 the Dutch historian Jan Romein wrote an essay called 'The Dialectics of Progress' in which he formulated his 'law of the handicap of the head start'. It basically states that any society loses the incentive to innovate further when it has established a working model that is superior to anything else at the time of its conception. As a famous example he used the fact that London was late in switching to electric street lighting since it was the first city with gas street lighting.

Harvard Business Professor Clayton Christensen in his many works reached a similar conclusion, albeit it from a company perspective. He found that although technological advances result in new products that fulfil the same function for a customer at a fraction of the cost (compared to the current generation they are meant to replace), manufacturers are reluctant to pursue such innovations. This is because they often mean lower price tags and lower margins, and thus leave the market open for new entrants that are happy with a lower level of profitability. In his view such 'disruption is a core micro-economic driver for macro-economic growth'.[16]

Taking these two views together we can argue that African companies are in an ideal position to develop next generation products and services (because the current generation is offered by Western companies at high prices and margins), and that African markets are the ideal places in which to launch them (because often the products and services they aim to replace barely or don't exist).

Take power as an example. Mostly due to economies of scale and scope, the power industry in developed countries is characterised by large power stations that supply electricity into the power grid, which supplies electricity to households and companies. But many assumptions that were the foundation of this industry no longer hold. Most importantly, we now have new and alternative ways to generate and distribute power on a much smaller scale, allowing for localised production, via, for example, photovoltaic cells and small wind farms. By going this route, we would have to dislodge the incumbent industry players in the West, which would be accompanied by large-scale job losses and massive capital destruction. In

Africa the picture is different – since many people have never been hooked up to the grid and the whole sector is woefully underdeveloped, we can start afresh.

Another example can be found in the Information and Communication Technology (ICT) sector. It is widely known that the mobile phone leapfrogged the landline in most countries in Africa, but a similar development is underway in the field of computing. Many Africans will never own a PC, but will instead access the Internet directly by using a smartphone. These are not just trends emerging by themselves, but the result of clever strategies that certain companies, such as MTN and Zain, are pursuing

As a matter of fact, many such opportunities exist in other areas where the network effect reigns (the idea that a product or service is only of value if many people use it, and they pay for the central infrastructure), such as power, sanitation, water, telecommunications, financial services, etc. Imagine if the poorer parts of Africa became the first place on Earth where hydrogen fuel would take root simply because there is limited fossil fuel infrastructure to replace.

Africa as an exporter

Despite the recent calls for more local 'beneficiation' of natural resources, a lot is to be said for adding value closer to the end user. So, while it may sound politically attractive to make steel in African countries for export, it does not make sense from an economic point of view due to the high logistics costs to transport the output to developed markets.

Only when the value of minerals is high compared to its volume (such as with gold and raw diamonds) and the logistics costs of the beneficiated product are low in comparison to its market value (such as with jewellery and polished diamonds) are there opportunities for beneficiation. However, such opportunities are limited, typically require very advanced skills and exist in imperfect (read difficult to penetrate) markets.

For export opportunities, let's look at two other resources that Africa has an abundance of: *terroir* (or local conditions, the growing environment) and people.

The 'food scare' of 2007/08 (where rising prices and export bans were imposed on producers) drove home the need for some countries to start worrying about food security. Exacerbated by water security, some nations are now looking at Africa to secure their future nutritional needs, and many big land acquisitions have recently been made, mostly by Asian and Middle Eastern countries.

As with many investments in Africa, this practice has attracted plenty of criticism. This is mostly related to the low prices paid for the land, and the concern that the agricultural exports will endanger the food security of the local population.

But think it through. Many parts of Africa have plenty of space, fertile soils, a perfect climate, and cultures adapted to agricultural work. In addition, recent technological breakthroughs have made the exploration of deep groundwater (which is widely available, especially near mountainous regions) commercially feasible. With the right investments and transfer of technology, large-scale agricultural enterprises can be established that create employment, generate export revenues and produce extra agricultural output for local consumption. It's a true win-win scenario.

A possibly even more controversial idea would be to transform the massive population growth in Africa into an advantage by developing its young people into export 'products'.

The populations of modernised countries are ageing rapidly, have high income levels, and needs that the younger quartile is loath to meet: jobs in (health) care, construction, public transport and the crafts, to mention a few, are ever harder to fill. At the same time, many young Africans would love to leave for such countries, but lack the necessary skills to land a decent job.

So, why not (as a business) set up colleges in Africa where young people learn a trade as well as the language and culture of the destination country so that on graduating they can be gainfully employed by households or organisations in the West? The idea is for them to serve abroad temporarily, learn extra skills, remit surplus income back to their families, and ultimately return to their home country to deploy their skills and experience for the benefit of the local economy.

Conclusion

I have sketched a very positive medium-term outlook for Africa. But in the short term, as a result of the global financial crisis, Africa will take strain. We will undoubtedly see an increase in civil strife and political instability and a degradation of living conditions for many.

My vision for Africa will only take shape if Africa's leadership continues to commit to good governance – as they have generally done for the past decade. But under current conditions the temptations or pressures to regress may be too high to withstand.

My most important argument is that companies need to take the leap into Africa now, and not wait until the economic situation improves, since the opportunities are many, the risks manageable and the competition still limited.

We would do well to note what esteemed Stanford economist Paul Romer once said: 'A crisis is a terrible thing to waste'.

Notes

1   Peter Schwartz, 'The African Time Machine'. *Red Herring*, November 2000.

2   Schwartz, 'The African Time Machine'.

3   Schwartz, 'The African Time Machine'.

4   Rutger-Jan van Spaandonk, 'SCP Africa Fund I and Sandhurst Capital Partners'. Sandhurst Capital Partners, October 2007.

5   'The G8 meets in Gleneagles, Scotland, [in July 2005] and pledges $50bn in development aid by 2010, with half going to Africa. Critics say the rich nations are still at least $15bn short of the target.' See George Parker and Guy Dinmore, 'Arguments over how Many to Invite to the Party'. *Financial Times*, 10 July 2009.

6   African Development Bank Group, *African Economic Outlook 2009*. Paris, 2009.

7   Sources include www.sars.gov.za/home.asp?pid=4232 (accessed 21 July 2009) and Rand Carlton analysis.

8   TED stands for Technology Education Design. The organisation, based in the USA, defines its mission as 'ideas worth spreading' and hosts an annual conference of leading global thinkers.

9   'Benjamin Zander on Music and Passion.' Video, www.ted.com/talks/lang/eng/benjamin_zander_on_music_and_passion.html (accessed 21 July 2009).

10 Vijay Mahajan develops an argument along similar lines in his book *Africa Rising: How 900 Million African Consumers Offer More than you Think* (Wharton School Publishing, 2008). But most of the reasoning here originated from my 2007 private equity fundraising initiative 'SCP Africa Fund I and Sandhurst Capital Partners'.

11 See www.worldbank.org (see Data, Quick Reference Tables) and Rand Carlton Analysis – data sets of 1 July 2009 (accessed 21 July 2009).

12 World Bank and Rand Carlton analysis.

13 Michael E. Porter, 'The Competitive Advantage of Nations'. *Harvard Business Review*, March–April 1990.

14 See the company website, www.pzcussons.com/pzc/ir/news_pres/pres2009/2009-01-27a/4885437.pdf (accessed 21 July 2009).

15 See the following companies' websites: PEP, www.pepstores.com (accessed 21 July 2009); Shoprite, www.shoprite.co.za/pages/127416071/About.asp (accessed 21 July 2009); and Woolworths, www.woolworths.co.za/Caissa.asp?Page=ITB4_RHConText&Post=CO-Stores_Franchise (accessed 21 July 2009).

16 Clayton Christensen, Thomas Craig and Stuart Hart, 'The Great Disruption'. *Foreign Affairs*, March–April 2001.

FLUX OBSERVATION

The culture of collaboration

Sarah Badat

COUNTLESS INDIVIDUALS have embraced an online culture defined by sharing, engaging with each other, collaborating and co-creating. And what happens online doesn't stay online with this growing community applying these values in offline life, demonstrating a new-found eagerness to share resources and information with each other. Likewise, brands are responding by introducing cross-industry collaborations and co-branding ventures that make good business sense in an uncertain economic climate.

Keeping in line with the general mood of sharing, the open source software movement has made access to information free for all, inspiring the rise of organised networks, both online and offline, with the purpose of pooling knowledge to increase collective intelligence. The global financial crisis has fast-tracked this phenomenon with tighter budgets and limited access to resources; consumers and brands everywhere are starting to embrace collaboration, finding comfort in the fact that we're all in this together.

Sharing as a business model

From co-branding and co-location strategies to partnerships, sponsorships and multi-branding ventures, more and more businesses are collaborating to share resources and cut costs in a time of budget constraints.

In June 2009, trends and innovation company PSFK hosted a

panel discussion on contemporary collaboration with Mike Brown of Virgin Group and Ben Lerer of Thrillist among the participants.[1] The discussion centred on the possibilities of creative collaboration in the realm of business and entrepreneurship and focused on how creative individuals and business entities can benefit from working around shared interests. A common sentiment emerged: that smaller creative groups and individuals need to leverage what they have over large companies via a bartering process of sorts. This would involve an exchange taking place between small firms that demonstrate technological and intellectual innovation and larger firms that have the resources to implement these ideas.

Apple has managed to design a successful collaborative business model with the launch of its iPhone Applications that allows business developers to collaborate with Apple to create applications that cater to the needs of iPhone users the world over. According to Forbes, Apple now offers more than 50 000 applications for the iPhone through its online App Store and in April, Apple announced that iPhone users had downloaded 1 billion applications online.[2]

This collaborative initiative means that suddenly content owners have the tools to create tailored interfaces and with the global reach of the iPhone they are able to connect and share their services with customers across geographic boundaries.

In June 2009 Apple partnered with car-sharing service Zipcar to create an application that allows users of Zipcar to find, reserve and even unlock vehicles using their iPhones. According to Zipcar CEO Luke Schneider: 'There is a synergy between the two brands. Before partnering with Apple, we polled a bunch of our customers and found out that about 25% of them are iPhone users',[3] which meant that tapping into the brand made sense from a practical perspective.

In addition to collaborating to pursue new business opportunities, there is a parallel movement that is seeing organisations and individuals embrace sharing as a means to participate in the global exchange of knowledge. Looking at the Forbes list of the 'Web Celeb 25' that ranked the 25 most influential personalities on the web today,[4] there is a common thread emerging. Influential personalities such as Guy Kawasaki, with his 'How to Change the World' blog, and Kevin Rose, founder of content-sharing site Digg, who both appear on the Forbes list, have made it their business to share all they know for free.

From a professional standpoint, sharing your latest and greatest ideas on the web could lead to a loss of competitive advantage, right? We need to rethink the notion that exclusivity equates to expertise.

At their best, online networking services have become unique centres for discussion and engagement through active participation and the open exchange of information. In June 2009 the United Nations announced the launch of the University of the People, the world's first tuition-free online university.[5] The school addresses the lack of higher education in developing countries and opens the gates to individuals who otherwise would not be able to afford tertiary education. Enrolled students are placed in classes of twenty, after which they log on to weekly lectures presented by voluntary lecturers, participate in discussions with their peers and take tests online. This unique university model acts as a platform to facilitate knowledge sharing and inspire the global exchange of information. Thinking along the same lines, YouTube recently launched YouTube Edu, an educational hub dedicated to providing free official lecture videos from over a hundred prestigious educational institutions, including Harvard Business School and MIT, which are part of a growing movement by academic institutions worldwide to offer free content online.[6]

Corporate generosity

Loren Phillips

Trendwatching.com published a report in 2009 on what it termed 'Generation G'. The 'G' stands for generosity and the report highlights individuals and companies that are choosing to give along with take.

This trend is clearly discernible in South Africa. One of the aspects the report deals with is 'personal philanthropy'. It lists a number of extremely High Net-Worth Individuals (HNWI), among them Bill Gates and Richard Branson, who generously donate their wealth, time and resources to a variety of causes. Locally there is Mark Shuttleworth who has helped develop 'Ubuntu', a free computer-operating system, as well as other forms of open-source software. In 2001 he established the Shuttleworth Foundation, a non-profit organisation dedicated to social innovation, which also funds free open-source educational software in South Africa.

The Trendwatching report highlights corporate community programmes, many examples of which are to be found locally. The MySchool programme ploughs profits from retailers back into communities. The programme has partnered with retailers across the board, such as Woolworths, Kalahari.net and Engen, to allow cardholders to contribute to a school or organisation of their choice, at no cost to themselves. According to Helene van Dyk, Communications and CSI Manager, MySchool has raised more than R82 million for schools and charities since its inception in 1998. Furthermore, every month one MySchool cardholder stands a chance to win R10 000 worth of products, which also wins an equal amount for the school of his or her choice. This is an excellent example of 'co-donation', one of the building blocks of corporate generosity.

There are other steps that caring companies can take besides helping people. One is to help care for the Earth through eco-responsibility projects. Pick 'n Pay, recognised globally as one of the top ten companies in the Carbon Disclosure Project, has committed to improving energy efficiency by 20% by 2012. It is firmly on track, having recently set up a wind-turbine project in Port Elizabeth that has been integrated into the power grid by the local municipality.

'This installation goes a long way in addressing the reality that we need to

TREND SNACK

Corporate generosity *continued*

rethink the way in which we operate in order to guarantee a sustainable future,' says Tessa Chamberlain, the company's General Manager of Sustainable Development.

We could argue that for too long people have been at the mercy of corporate agendas and that the consumer is now beginning to want a say in how things get done. Corporate generosity, including the various elements of empowering communities, co-donation and eco-generosity, is a response to this shift in the mindset of consumers. It signifies a fundamental shift in the way companies will run in the future.

T R E N D S N A C K

Push opportunities, not only products

With consumers starting to expect more than products from their brands, it is becoming increasingly important for companies to explore means of offering them ways to participate, share and collaborate, especially when it comes to corporate social investment. It is no longer enough for brands to stand back and simply push a product that has little meaning or personal worth to consumers. By implementing sharing as a core business value, brands are able to link opportunities to products and services, giving customers a richer, more memorable experience along with the satisfaction of contributing to a better world for all.

Mobile Movement, a Canadian initiative in collaboration with UN-Habitat, Microsoft Research India and the Environmental Youth Alliance provides mobile phones to young entrepreneurs in developing countries.[7] Its first project is under way in Kenya and features fifteen youth groups with business ideas that are being taught how to send texts, emails and take photos to facilitate the growth of their businesses. Interested sponsors can check out the group profiles on the Mobile Movement website and if they find one that interests them, they can post a comment which is sent directly to the group's phone. The group then responds via email or text message and so begins a global business conversation. Donors can offer creative business suggestions or mentoring as well as micro-financing loans. Several groups have already received funding and a creative business partnership was formed between a bone-craft collective in Nairobi and New York-based jewellery designer, Olia Gitman.

Tell us what you know

It seems that when days are dark, friends can in fact be found everywhere. Online networks that facilitate the sharing of advice, reviews and resources have helped consumers acquire peace of mind before they commit to a brand or product offering. The general movement towards helping each other out in whatever way possible has allowed consumers to join forces and demonstrate their power to make a difference to the lives of others. In both real world meet-ups and online forums, people are coming together to solve problems, give advice, answer questions and share insights.

Social search engines and review sites have made it possible for almost anyone to share and access online reviews but more and more people are looking closer to home for advice from people within their own network. San Francisco start-up Aardvark has taken general review sites a step further by getting more personally relevant information from a user's own networks of friends.[8] Users of Aardvark begin by adding the service to their email or Instant Messaging (IM) friend list and then sending the system a question – for example, about a recommendation for 'great music' or a 'hotel room in Paris'. Aardvark then checks the user's social network of participating friends and friends-of-friends to see who can answer it. After narrowing in on a small group of the user's social network, Aardvark finds someone who can answer the question in real time and, within minutes, sends the answer back to the person who asked for it.

Using online services to facilitate sharing between personal networks highlights the shifting paradigm of how people are gathering and exchanging information. Instead of simply relying on the mounds of information provided by traditional search engines like Google, people are experimenting with services that offer subjective, customised answers based on the opinions of people they know and trust.

In an article that appeared in *The New York Times* Malia Wollan proposes: 'If YouTube can illustrate how to solve a Rubik's Cube, pick a lock and poach an egg, maybe it can also demonstrate how to give birth.'[9] Wollan is referring to the growing number of mothers posting their home-birth videos on YouTube for other expectant mothers to watch and learn from. These women are opening up a dialogue with viewers by responding to their questions and comments and thereby helping to better inform them before their own birth experience. This shows a changing dynamic of information-sharing that is solely for the benefit of others.

From sharing home-birthing videos to community produce sharing initiatives and ride-sharing programmes, consumers are now more than ever showing a willingness to share what they have and what they know to help others. UK-based Landshare has launched a garden-sharing scheme that puts would-be gardeners who lack garden space in contact with those who would like to see their underutilised land put to good use.[10]

American organisation VeggieTrader works on a similar principle, connecting users through the exchange of fruit and vegetables. All over the USA, the fruit-sharing movement is growing, with sites like neighborhoodfruit.com and fallenfruit.org allowing people to share and source produce in an online forum that represents a virtual farmers' market.[11]

Fruit sharing has now moved offline with communities and neighborhoods hosting their own produce exchanges, illustrating the power of social networks to bring people together in real world meet-ups, build communities of interest and inspire change.

The recession has played a key role in bringing about creative ways of sharing. Job sharing in the workplace, whereby employees opt to share working hours to avoid retrenchment, has found currency in corporate Japan with auto companies including Toyota, Isuzu and Mitsubishi Motors embracing work sharing as a means of cutting costs whilst maintaining the image of social responsibility during the downturn. The Japanese job-sharing phenomenon has been traced back to rural communities, such as Himeshima, where work sharing has been commonplace for decades. Residents of this tiny coastal island sacrifice wages and regular working hours for the sake of keeping everybody in the community employed. Japan's Labour Minister Yoichi Masuzoe described job sharing as a 'revolutionary concept' and a source of worker solidarity in the dire economic climate.[12]

American-based Zimride has launched a free online carpool community that allows registered users to search for rides with people sharing their route. If they find a match in the search engine, users can opt to join the available ride to lower their commuting costs and reduce their carbon footprint. Zimriders can check the profiles of those offering rides for common networks, interests and friends, before deciding to share. The site's founders hope that ride sharing will become a social activity that allows users to connect and establish relationships based on social trust.[13]

As we begin to understand the impact of the global sharing of knowledge and resources we can see that what started as an online movement is increasingly manifesting itself in offline life – the result is the creation and development of communities that are mobilised and actively engaging in various forms of networking. In the long run, sharing information will benefit us all by increasing our collective pool of knowledge, thereby providing greater opportunities for innovation.

We simply need to consider the contexts of where sharing is taking place and realise that building environments – whether on-line or in the real world – that facilitate sharing and collaboration represents the most authentic sign of expertise that there is.

Notes

1 PSFK Good Ideas Salon hosted by Piers Fawkes, 5 June 2009, Art Directors Club, New York City. See www.psfk.com (accessed 29 June 2009).

2 Brian Caulfield, 'IPhone Apps Turn the Web on its Head'. Forbes.com, 12 June 2009, www.forbes.com/2009/06/12/iphone-apple-mobile-technology-personal-tech-iphone.html (accessed 29 June 2009).

3 Ben Mack, 'Zipcar iPhone App Makes Car-Sharing a Breeze'. Wired.com, 10 June 2009, www.wired.com/autopia/2009/06/zipcar-iphone/ (accessed 29 June 2009).

4 David Ewalt and Michael Noer, 'The Web Celeb 25'. Forbes.com, 29 January 2009, www.forbes.com/2009/01/29/web-celebrities-internet-technology-webceleb09_0129_land.html (accessed 29 June 2009).

5 See University of the People, www.uopeople.org (accessed 29 June 2009).

6 Andrea Ford, 'Logging on to the Ivy League'. *Time*, 16 April 2009.

7 See Mobile Movement, www.mobilemovement.tv (accessed 29 June 2009).

8 See Ardvark, www.vark.com (accessed 29 June 2009).

9 Malia Wollan, 'Lights, Camera, Contraction!' *The New York Times*, 10 June 2009.

10 See Landshare, www.landshare.org (accessed 29 June 2009).

11 Kim Severson, 'Neighbour, can you Spare a Plum?' *The New York Times*, 9 June 2009.

12 Leo Lewis, 'Tactics for Hard Times as Japanese Turn to Job Sharing'. Times Online, 17 January 2009, www.timesonline.co.uk/tol/news/world/asia/article5533117.ece (accessed 29 June 2009).

13 See Zimride, www.zimride.com (accessed 29 June 2009).

The newspaper may be dying: Long live news

Are we witnessing the slow death of print media?*

Irwin Manoim

Irwin Manoim worked in the media industry for 35 years before taking time off for a sabbatical near Silicon Valley, California, where he watched the online media revolution from a front-row seat. He was co-founder and editor of the *Weekly Mail* (now *Mail & Guardian*) and of the Electronic Mail & Guardian, the earliest online news operation in Africa. Manoim was also the first person to work online as a journalist in South Africa. For the past decade he has been a partner in the web development agency Big Media and a newspaper consultant helping to conceptualise new titles and advising on design and content strategies. He is a frequent public speaker on media issues and also teaches post-graduate students at the Journalism Department of the University of the Witwatersrand in Johannesburg.

JUNE 2007. The grandees of the world's newspaper industry gather in Cape Town for a few days of golf, sightseeing and checking up on what the other guys are doing. In between trips to Stellenbosch, and some hobnobbing with Nelson Mandela and the newly ascending Jacob Zuma, spirits are high. The global newspaper industry is in better health than ever. As the keynote address at the 60th World Newspaper Congress points out, the total circulation of newspapers around the world has gone up nearly 10% in five years. Revenues are up 15.77% over five years. As the last slide, in a procession of many, puts it: 'Newspapers are a growth business!'[1]

*   *   *

June 2009. I brace myself for a solemn pilgrimage to an American website whose single purpose is to commemorate the death of newspapers. The site consists of a map of the USA, dotted with black pins, one for each deceased title. On my first visit, early in 2009, there are some 20 pins. When I come back a fortnight later, the number has reached 25. Most of the newspapers I've never heard of,[2] but a few I have: *The Christian Science Monitor*, *The Rocky Mountain News*, the *Seattle Post Intelligencer* and the *Baltimore Examiner*.[3] I keep returning. The number reaches 30, then 35. By May, there are 40 pins. I visit again in early June. The site has collapsed. There are too many pins.[4]

An imploding industry

What happened in two years? How did this industry implode so quickly, so unexpectedly? The first, obvious culprit is the global recession. As currencies slipped, paper prices rose. Advertising revenues collapsed. Once-confident media empires found themselves overstretched. Employees of *The New York Times*, which only recently moved into a much-admired and rather expensive avant-garde building, awoke one morning to discover that the Old Grey Lady was unable to pay a US$1.1 billion debt. In Illinois, a cocky billionaire property dealer who bought the *Chicago Tribune* and *Los Angeles Times* on the cheap found himself, not many months later, in a bankruptcy court.

Some cities seemed on the verge of losing all their newspapers: Los Angeles, Boston, Detroit, San Francisco, Miami, Denver and Newark. Across the Atlantic, Irish rugby-hero-turned-tycoon Sir Anthony O'Reilly, owner of scores of newspapers and magazines around the world – including seventeen major dailies and weeklies in South Africa – lost his job as his company faced hostile shareholders and an R18 billion debt. In France, President Nicolas Sarkozy suggested a national scheme to provide every eighteen year old with a free one-year newspaper subscription.

In London, the market research company Group M warned in December 2008 that advertising in 2009 would be down 15%. In March 2009 it revised that figure down to 20%. In June it revised it down again to 23%, and added the warning that dozens of newspaper and magazine titles were 'under lethal threat'.[5]

But it is not the recession that the print industry fears. The monster that lurks in the shadows is the Internet. Over the past decade,

A glossy downturn

Carina Louw

When the belt being tightened is labelled Prada and *the* fashion bible American Vogue records unprecedented advertising and sales losses, you know that the glossy magazine industry is facing a crisis of enormous proportions.

The impact of the global financial meltdown on fashion magazines has been severe but it has also revealed a number of problems that have been festering beneath the glossy covers for some time. Industry critics say that many magazines are simply out of touch with the cultural changes that social networks and online media have brought about. Besides the radical drop in ad pages, many magazines have not evolved in a significant way and have grown stagnant from too much repetition of the same celebrity images, cover lines and topics year in and year out.

The recent proliferation and extreme popularity of personal style blogs, such as Childhood Flames, Sea of Shoes and Fashion Toast, is also slicing away at magazine sales and status. The blogs often feature a mix of high-end and budget fashion, something quite unheard of in the high fashion realm, as well as vintage labels. The massive hit rates on style blogs seem to indicate that many women would rather look at blogs featuring their peers for free than fork out on fashion spreads. The decline in sales is exacerbated by the fact that digital natives are less paper-dependent than their older print-everything counterparts in keeping with the global awareness of limited resources that the information age has spurned.

In recent years content has increasingly moved online, creating a culture in which consumers expect to get information for free. This would include receiving their glossies in the form of a contribution-based Portable Document Format (PDF) magazine – in which content is created for free by various contributors not employed by the magazine.

It has become a case of survival of the fittest as glossies the world over are trying to reinvent themselves. Companies Lexus, Time and American Express Publishing are giving readers a new way to customise their own personalised magazine. Called *Mine Magazine,* the free magazine invites readers to choose editorial content that interests them, which is then printed – complete with advertising

TREND SNACK

A glossy downturn *continued*

tailored for the individual reader. Although the content is free, magazines are waking up to the notion that people want increasing customisation and are more willing to pay for content that is specific and relevant.

In the USA *Marie Claire* recently launched a reality show that gives the public an insider's view of the day-to-day activities of an intern at a large fashion magazine. Meanwhile, American Vogue is getting attention for the award-winning documentary called 'The September Issue' that features Anna Wintour and her staff compiling the thickest issue of *Vogue* ever. Magazines are hoping that by generating more publicity they will be able to reach an audience that is increasingly unconvinced that a designer handbag is worth the price tag of R10 000. In the process, they are aiming to bring back the magic and excitement that used to be associated with fashion magazines.

The key to the future survival of glossies is to become hybridised. They need to fuse the physical appeal of print with the power to deliver online video, sound and other multi-media content that relies on more than just one of the senses. Moreover, with the world teetering on the edge of an economic precipice today, people will want to only pay for content that is authentic, relevant and inspiring.

T R E N D   S N A C K

the Internet has scored damaging blows against the two central pillars of the print industry. Firstly, it has taken away readers, particularly younger readers. Back in 1993, some 58% of the USA population read a newspaper every day. By 2008 that figure had dropped to 34%. Less than 2% of Americans used the Internet for news in 1995, but by 2008, the figure was 37%, slightly higher than the number reading printed newspapers.[6] While older people are still reading newspapers, the bad news is that younger people are hardly bothering to start. The same survey said that 44% of college graduates now read their news online. Why? The reason people give is invariably this: why pay for something when you can get it for free?

The second impact of the Internet is that it has taken away classified advertising, said to be worth over US$100 billion worldwide.[7] Classifieds have been the lifeblood of most daily newspapers ever since TV snatched away the more glamorous forms of national advertising. Today, 40% of newspaper revenues typically come from classified advertising.[8] The Newspaper Association of America says that in the third quarter of 2008, classified advertising across the country was down 30.85% to US$2.36 billion. That's not a dip. It's a mauling. (The figures were released in December 2008 and not long after, the Newspaper Association itself retrenched half of its staff.)

How did the Internet manage to steal away so much classified advertising?

It happened almost by accident. The most quoted example is Craigslist, which started as a one-man San Francisco community noticeboard, with an appealingly amateurish and anti-establishment feel, on which anyone could list anything, legal or otherwise, and the only taboo was money. Somehow, its fame spread. Four years later, Craigslist had crossed the USA; ten years on, and it is now available in local editions in almost every country on Earth, South Africa included. When Craigslist reached its fifth birthday, a consultant in the classified advertising business estimated that it had cost the newspapers in its home town of San Francisco some US$65 million in lost revenue.[9]

In both cases, the Internet has undermined print in the same simple way: by offering for free services that previously cost money.[10]

The local scene

Let's detour back to South Africa. On the one hand, we are always a little behind; on the other, we are sometimes ahead. Many of the desperate moves taking place abroad in recent months, such as rival titles agreeing to share buildings, printing presses and distribution systems, happened here years ago. No major South African newspaper has closed. But that's due to an optical illusion. The two major newspaper and magazine companies, Media24 (a reincarnation of the old Nasionale Pers) and Independent News and Media (owned by O'Reilly's ailing Irish multinational)[11] have solved their problems by administrative means. They have each cut back, de facto if not *de jure*, to a single news operation. But here's the cunning part: readers don't know, because the single newspaper appears in different editions in different cities under different titles. To make way for this efficiency, there has been a wave of retrenchments across both groups.

There's a twist to this tale. Total newspaper sales in South Africa have actually been going up for the past five years. The reason is that brash mass-market tabloids aimed at a black working-class readership have proved hugely successful. The *Daily Sun*, for example, powered by tales of the *tokoloshe* and lots of bloodshed, sells more than half a million papers a day, and is read by 5 million people, which more than makes up for the circulation lost by other, more staid newspapers.

This trend is not unique to South Africa. All over the Third World, but particularly in India and China, newspapers similar to the *Daily Sun* are selling millions of copies a day. One reason is that literacy levels, although not high, have risen just enough to encourage tabloid newspaper reading. Another is that authoritarian governments no longer try to own the press (an expensive way to lose money) but will allow commercial publishers fairly free rein – as long as they stay clear of politics. Thus, while print dies in the First World, it thrives, for now, in the Third. Indeed, sales of printing presses have never been more brisk.

News junkies

Have the easily distracted consumer classes of the USA and Europe suddenly lost interest in the hard work of reading the news? Not at all. The World Association of Newspapers was correct: more people are reading more news than ever before. The younger generation, the key to any industry's health, has become news junkies in a way that a previous generation became TV junkies.

Newspaper websites are winning readers faster than print is losing them. *The New York Times*, for example, has around 1 million daily print sales, and falling. Online, it has 20 million readers per month, and climbing.[12] In South Africa, three sites have long topped the website audience rankings, way ahead of any rivals. Two are newspaper sites: News24 (the online arm of Media24) and IOL (the online arm of Independent Newspapers). The third is MWEB, an Internet Service Provider site owned by a newspaper company (Naspers).

But for all that, newspaper proprietors are not celebrating. They have encountered an unexpected online competitor, known by the ugly nickname 'blog', short for 'weblog'. Blogs are rudimentary DIY websites, reminiscent of personal diaries, whose genius is that they can be managed by the technically clueless.

Bloggers are happiest when arguing from one blog to another, and they allow anyone else to join in the quarrels, which can be arcane and heated. Estimates as to the number of bloggers on the planet vary from 113 million to 184 million; in short, there are enough to populate several large countries.

Most blogs are unspeakably awful, as, no doubt, are most personal diaries. But a tiny minority, say, just a few hundreds of thousands, have proved good enough to shake the establishment media. The best blogs focus single-mindedly on a narrow area of interest. The blogger is often an expert in that field; perhaps *the* expert. The blog will attract the other experts to debate issues. As a result, a good blog can carry greater authority in its field than anything in the print media.

Blogs carry the most astonishing diversity of opinion, more than you may have ever imagined possible. Chance encounters with some of these can be enough to shake up your own comfortable assumptions. The print media, by contrast, have for decades been accused of airing only the narrowest range of opinions. It took the age of the blog to prove the point.

One of the most extraordinary features of the Internet has been the persistence of the ethos of 'free'. Historians of cyberspace trace this all the way back to the Internet's beginnings in the California counter-culture of the 1960s.[13] This happy idea is best exemplified by the free-for-all online encyclopaedia Wikipedia, for which thousands offer their time and expertise without expectation of payment. Indeed, apostles of the Internet have proclaimed free content the cornerstone of Internet culture.

Apostles of the Internet tend, alas, to imagine that cyberspace has escaped the shackles of a capitalist economy. The reason that free persists is not a widely shared belief in computing as personal liberation. Powerful interests stand to gain from maximising free Internet access. Microsoft, for example, whose money comes from the software that allows you to visit all those free sites, Internet Service Providers, search engines, telecoms companies, e-marketers, bloggers ... the list of those who profit by free content is a long one.

A number of other institutions are less happy with the ethos of free. One of them is the news business. What really rankles media executives is the realisation that other people *are* making money from their free content. Every time you read an article on *The New York Times*, a little fee is going, quietly and invisibly, to your Internet Service Provider, another fee goes to Telkom, and other little fees are being scattered among a host of ghostly electronic intermediaries between you and *The New York Times* website. Your 'free read' is actually costing you, but the price is hidden inside your monthly subscription to your Internet Service Provider.

A fierce debate rages on the subject of how the printed media can salvage themselves by making money online. The debate is hampered by the lack of a single convincing example of a print media company earning its keep online. On one side of the debate are those who have great faith in the power of online advertising revenues; on the other side, those who don't. Advertising, after all, powers other thriving free media, including TV, radio and community 'knock 'n drop' papers. The Internet advertising sector began rather shakily, unable to convince clients that it could deliver results. Then suddenly, around 2005, it took off, zipping well ahead of radio advertising. In Britain, for example, online advertising rose 40% in the year 2006 alone, and was expected to catch up to TV advertising by the end of 2010.[14]

But there's a snag. In the world of print, newspapers and magazines rule a well-fenced domain. In cyberspace, the news media have to compete with ... *everyone*. Every listing site, every travel site, every games site or blog, can carry advertising.

One-fifth of online advertising revenue goes to 'community'

websites, a category that covers the likes of Facebook, Craigslist and Yelp. Some 17% goes to search engines. Around 11% goes to email websites, and about the same goes to sports websites and to financial institutions. Then there are the news websites. They get 12%. Or, to put it another way: the news websites are not getting 88% of the online advertising cash pile. Worse, they are not getting much of their 12% slice either: the biggest bites go to broadcasters such as CNN, or 'news aggregators' such as AOL news or Yahoo news.[15]

Newspapers are hugely expensive operations. A printing press costs much the same as your average Boeing 747. The high price has always suited the industry; it has kept competitors at bay. Some 14% of newspaper operating costs typically go to editorial, and 16% to advertising. The remaining 70% of costs covers paper and printing, distribution, rent and other corporate functions.[16] If newspapers were to stop their print editions and boldly move online, it would be possible to cut much of that 70%. But the operation would still cost more than it could earn from online advertising revenue. A report by PricewaterhouseCoopers estimated that in 2007 online revenues typically made up 7% of advertising revenue for newspapers and forecast that the figure would reach 15% by 2012. And that modest figure came before the recession.[17]

These figures explain why print executives believe that they will not make money online unless they can persuade readers to pay in some form. The former managing editor of *Time* magazine, Walter Isaacson, caused a stir with an article calling for a 'micro-payment' system in which users are charged small amounts of money each time they access an article. He pointed out that the music industry has managed to turn what was a losing battle against piracy into an effective pay-per-tune download model, and that social networks such as Facebook and Twitter have their own micro-payment schemes.

In April 2009 three prominent former newspaper executives went a step further than Isaacson, actually forming their own company to devise a system that allows readers to buy a 'pass' that covers any participating website.[18] Each time a visitor arrives at a site, a small payment is invisibly recorded. A similar system is called Kachingle, which also offers a pass to any participating website, but works on the basis of voluntary donations.[19] By the time you read this, a winning system may have emerged.

The rise of the blogger

It's time now to confront the monster, the big 'what if' question. What if, sometime not far off, you were to walk into your local café, look around for a newspaper or magazine, and be told: 'Sorry, nobody publishes those any more.' Would it be a terrible thing? Many people think so. In fact, the past few months have been rather like witnessing the slow death of a much-disliked uncle: only when his end is nigh do you suddenly become aware of his virtues. People who complained about how unpleasant newspapers were to read, smearing ink all over their bedsheets and tablecloths, have now discovered how 'user-friendly' they are. People who complained of sensationalism, inaccuracy and superficiality, are now troubled by the disappearance of the public's watchdog. Who will cover city council meetings? Who will send live human beings into war zones?

To answer this, we need first to separate the newspaper from the journalism. They are not at all the same. Newspaper proprietors have had various motives – vanity and ideology among them – but most modern newspaper corporations are in the business of providing a medium for advertising. To work as an advertising medium, a newspaper needs an audience. Journalism has proved to be one of the better hooks to an audience, but there are plenty of others: competitions, crossword puzzles, racing results and movie listings. There is no relationship between quality of journalism and quantity of revenue; indeed, great journalism tends to be an estranged relative of profit.

Nor do newspapers provide a nurturing environment for journalism. The pressure to sell newspapers encourages sensationalism; the artificial device of the 'deadline' encourages haste. It takes a brave and foolish editor to question the practices of a major advertiser. In fact, the best journalism is only sporadically to be found in newspapers. It is more consistently found in text-heavy periodicals such as the *New Yorker*, *Atlantic* or *Harper's* – rare institutions that can afford to allow a journalist six months to study a single topic. Or it is found in non-fiction books, the kind that serious journalists feel compelled to write as an escape from the newsroom.[20]

If newspapers and magazines were to die, there is little doubt that the likely replacement would be websites such as blogs. Internet advertising may not yet sustain a newsroom, but it is already enough to provide an individual with a welcome second income. The big question is whether these online publications would provide journalism of quality. The 'blogger in his pyjamas'[21] has plenty of opinions, but can he or she do hard, slog reporting? Below are some of the issues this raises.

Can an individual blogger be trusted?

An institution such as a newspaper does at least have a reputation, reinforced by a system of editorial oversights. An individual blogger of no reputation will have to earn a reputation in sweat and time,

Drunk on free love

Sarah Badat

In the pursuit of a new model for news media, charging readers micro-payments for content seems like a grand idea. But what happens when those readers, who are so used to receiving content for free, can't come to terms with actually having to pay for it? Add to this the dwindling number of advertisers due to recession-induced budget cuts and it becomes clear that the publishing industry is standing on a slippery slope.

The war for the almost saturated attention of consumers has resulted in news publications merrily giving away free love to attract readers. A study done by Pew Research Center found that 2008 was the tipping point for print media as more people in the USA got their news online for free than by paying for newspapers and magazines.

According to Newspaper Innovation, an organisation concerned with tracking free daily newspapers, there are more than 1 678 545 sites that offer free news, and by the end of 2008 there were free newspapers in 58 countries with a daily readership of more than 70 million readers.

Savvy consumers are realising that free no longer means inferior quality and younger generations who see charging for web content as 'evil' are growing up expecting an increasing number of goods and services to be free. The explosion of 'try before you buy' marketing has made consumers doubt the benefits of buying at all. It makes no sense, for example, to pay for a subscription to *The New York Times* when the entire paper can be delivered to your inbox for free every morning with additional breaking news headlines appearing as they happen. The plan to entice news readers with a bit of free content seems to be the Achilles heel of the publishing industry.

With the help of various online tools, more consumers are becoming producers of free news themselves and they are expecting the same free-for-all model from news organisations. Beyond the realm of print media free love is spreading. The open source software movement has inspired initiatives like Mark Shuttleworth's Ubuntu free operating system software, while social media sites like Twitter and Facebook give their users a free medium to share and access information. Even offline companies are handing out freebies left, right and centre, from Wimpy's free coffee on voting day to Ben & Jerry's free ice-cream cone day, proving how giving free love is becoming an essential part of doing business.

Reference: Newspaper Innovation, www.newspaperinnovation.com (accessed 29 June 2009).

like anyone else. Most will never get there. But some bloggers arrive with reputations and they have become bloggers precisely because they are experts.

Can bloggers cover the dull stuff?

At a USA Senate hearing on the future of newspapers in May 2009, an editor remarked that the great value of newspapers is in the recording of the small, dull, but important minutiae of ordinary life. The example he provided was coverage of city hall meetings. A blogger then responded, providing a list of more than a dozen amateur blogs in the editor's home town that, between them, covered city hall far more thoroughly than his newspaper.[22] Blogs tend to operate on the swarm principle. Where there's an issue, scores of enthusiasts will descend upon it. Some will know the technicalities of an issue better than any journalist can hope to. But others will be partisan, perhaps dangerously so.

Can bloggers do investigations?

Investigative reporting is the elite corps of the profession, the work that makes journalists feel good about journalism. Can amateurs seriously compete? In fact, amateurs have a surprisingly good record. The now almost-forgotten Bill Clinton–Monica Lewinsky affair first appeared on a scruffy website called The Drudge Report. The 'waterboarding' torture allegations that made headlines for much of 2009, started life on the blog of a woman named Marcy Wheeler who, unlike scores of professional journalists, read a series of recently released Justice Department memos very carefully.[23] During the interminable USA elections marathon, hardly a week went by when some blogger did not shame the news establishment. Investigative reporting requires courage, persistence, time, some luck and an obsessive personality, all of which are available to amateurs; but also money and manpower, which seldom are. So there are likely to be some kinds of investigations that only institutions with resources can accomplish.

Can bloggers cover wars or uprisings?

Wars are another glory area, but one in which newspapers have a sorrier record than they will admit. Journalists tend to be denied first-hand access to battle zones and are obliged to rely on propagandists from the warring factions, making them easy prey for manipulation. The bloggers who break stories during wars are quite often the people on the ground, eyewitnesses to history. Their opinions may be as partisan as anyone else's in a war zone, but just being there gives them an advantage reporters don't enjoy. However, when it comes to wars, caution is the watchword, regardless.

*   *   *

We probably have a few more years to sort through these arguments. The current shake-out of titles matches what happened when TV first mauled the industry. In almost every city, at least one title died, providing space for the remaining titles to survive and even prosper. When the *Rand Daily Mail* died in 1985, ten years after TV reached South Africa, the *Star* and *Sowetan* flourished. Should the debt-ridden *New York Times* actually expire, the *Wall Street Journal* will move into its territory. Modern digital printing methods make it possible for newspapers to expand way beyond their traditional home-town turf. It is already possible to buy the latest edition of the London *Financial Times* every day in Johannesburg. The danger to local titles is that geography no longer insulates them against predators from abroad.

But the big action will move increasingly online. The old distinction between newspapers and magazines – one printed at frequent intervals on cheap paper, one printed less often on expensive paper – will vanish. A magazine website and a newspaper website are one and the same. Instead, there will be distinctions between hand-held mobile devices offering rapid-fire news in short bursts, and large-screen devices offering more sustained reading. But even these distinctions may be temporary. Amazon's Kindle, a hand-held electronic device resembling an oversized cellphone, may be the early precursor of a device small enough to be portable, but large enough to allow comfortable reading.[24]

And what of the bloggers, now sniffing their moment of triumph? The wonder of blogs is that there are so many of them, and that their only driver is personal commitment. Can this last? It is a characteristic of infant markets that there are huge numbers of competing brands, none of which achieves dominance. One day, a Bill Gates figure arrives and finds the hidden treasure. Then consolidation begins. Brands are swallowed up or stomped on by other brands, cartels form, the rich get richer and the poor fall by the wayside.[25] Once there were many search engines; now there are Google and Yahoo and the dwarves. A multitude of blogs will not replace the news establishment. A handful of blogs will become the news establishment. The blogger in his pyjamas will morph into the blogger in his dark suit, employer of scores of minions, his website driven by a need to please the advertisers, beat the competition and titillate ever-larger audiences. The future will have a comforting familiarity.

Notes

* The media terrain has been in turmoil in recent months and a number of events have occurred since this article was completed at the beginning of June 2009. Nevertheless, the overall picture described here remains valid.

1 Timothy Baldwin, CEO of the World Association of Newspapers, gave the keynote address at the 60th World Newspaper Congress held in Cape Town, in June 2007.

2 A random selection of small-town American titles included: *Algonquin Countryside*, *Cary-Grove Countryside*, *Wauconda Courier*, and *American Fork Citizen*. The list goes on.

3 Some of these still exist, for now, in online-only form, but their print editions have been closed.

4 See Paper Cuts, www.graphicdesignr.net/papercuts (accessed 3 June 2009). The site also keeps a tally of American journalists who have been retrenched. From August to December 2007: 2 112; from January to December 2008: 15 970; and, from January to May 2009: 10 025.

5 Mark Sweney, 'Magazines and Newspapers Face "Lethal Threat" from Advertising Downturn'. Guardian Online, 3 June 2009, www.guardian.co.uk/media/2009/jun/03/group-m-magazines-newspapers-lethal-threat (accessed 3 June 2009).

6 Pew Research Center for the People and the Press, August 2008, www.pewresearch.org (accessed 3 June 2009).

7 Eric Pfanner, 'Craigslist Circles the Globe with Online Classifieds, One City at a Time'. *International Herald Tribune*, 17 January 2005, www.nytimes.com/2005/01/17/technology/17craigslist.html?_r=1 (accessed 3 June 2009).

8 This is the average, according to the Newspaper Association of America.

9 Pfanner, 'Craigslist Circles the Globe'.

10 I refer chiefly to daily newspapers, because that is the industry sector in the most immediate trouble. The magazine industry, which is particularly dependent on young readers, is in similar circumstances. And for that matter, so is TV. But that's another article entirely.

11 Independent News and Media's debt crisis had not been resolved when this article was completed in early June. There was a fear that it could spill over into its South African holdings.

12 The comparison should be treated with some caution, since different methods are used to define print and online readers.

13 See Fred Turner, *From Counterculture to Cyberculture* (University of Chicago Press, 2006), which traces this history through the Whole Earth Catalog, the online

debating forum WELL, and the bedroom computer hobbyists who invented personal computing.

14 Amanda Andrews, 'Online Spend Forecast to Pass TV'. Times Online, 5 October 2006. According to Andrews: 'The chief executive of the Internet Advertising Bureau, Guy Phillipson … said that by the end of this year the Internet advertising market will be worth £2 billion and is expected to overtake national press advertising', www.business.timesonline.co.uk/tol/business/industry_sectors/media/article660590.ece (accessed 3 June 2009).

15 Based on the Nielsen Online ratings for USA usage, April 2009.

16 According to a report by Moody's Investors Service, 4 June 2009.

17 PricewaterhouseCoopers' Global Entertainment and Media Outlook, 2008.

18 Called Journalism Online and founded by Steve Brill, Leo Hindery and Gordon Crovitz.

19 Described by Steve Outing in 'Forget Micro-payments: Here's a Far Better Idea for Monetizing Content', 10 February 2009, www.editorandpublisher.com/eandp/columns/stopthepresses_display.jsp?vnu_content_id=1003940234 (accessed 3 June 2009).

20 Newspapers do indeed have moments of glory. But the best journalism in South Africa tends, consistently, to be found in documentary books researched at length and leisure by former reporters such as Jonny Steinberg, Mark Gevisser and Liz McGregor, for example.

21 A much-used metaphor these days. I first heard it mentioned by US columnist Michael Kinsley, former editor of Slate, at a New America Foundation panel on the newspaper crisis, May 2009.

22 A tale recounted at the same New America Foundation panel on the newspaper crisis, by Phil Bronstein, Executive Vice-President of the Hearst Corporation.

23 A close study of Marcy Wheeler's CV reveals no sign that she has ever worked as a journalist. Her blog, emptywheel, can be found at www.emptywheel.firedoglake.com (accessed 3 June 2009).

24 Amazon has an eye on the news market and has made preliminary deals with some publishers. The company has even released a larger version of its device, intended for news reading. But publishers have been slow to queue up, complaining that Amazon wants to charge them too much.

25 The day Craigslist announced that it would start charging for certain categories of advertising – mainly for the sex and jobs adverts – was the day the age of innocence developed its first wrinkle.

Where word of mouse rules

Is PR the new advertising?

Damon Stapleton

Damon Stapleton is Executive Creative Director at TBWA Hunt Lascaris. He had an eclectic childhood that included sixteen schools (only expelled twice). This has been matched by his career, which has seen him being a photographer, writer, film director, bad bartender and, finally, doing the respectable job of advertising. He has won many awards including a D&AD Yellow Pencil and the Cannes Lion Grand Prix.

They now sit in a beautiful cardboard box.

He is passionate about the need to eradicate people with five-year plans, Tuscan villas and anyone called Craig who wears chinos. He is also passionate about where advertising is going and if it will still be called advertising. It is this that made him get off the couch and write 'Where word of mouse rules'.

ON THE ceiling of the Hauptbahnhof train station in Cologne, Germany, is a work of art reminiscent of the Sistine Chapel. Visitors pour into the station to view it as they would any tourist attraction. While some may consider it a masterpiece, by its humblest definition, it is an advert.

Commissioned by Adidas for the 2006 FIFA World Cup, it is an 800-square-metre ode to soccer, featuring the likes of Beckham, Kaka and other World Cup 2006 football gods signed to the Adidas label. But unlike an advert you might see on TV or in a magazine, this one can't be switched off or tuned out, and it most certainly can't be forgotten. The reason this advert has created such an impression all around the world, let alone with the people who've seen it for themselves, is because it doesn't interrupt what they are interested in, it *is* what they are interested in.

Don't interrupt, entertain

For years advertising has counted on its ability to interrupt people while they are in a good headspace. While watching their favourite TV programme, in sneaks an advert to inform and, hopefully, entertain before the viewer has a chance to reach for the remote control. While reading a magazine, an advert that happens to sell a product they might be interested in is subtly slipped in somewhere between an article on better sex techniques and an interview with

Reese Witherspoon. Some have considered it insidious. We advertising folk have considered it good marketing.

But times are changing. For a start, people don't have to watch adverts any more. The introduction of the Personal Video Recorder (PVR) with its functionality allowing for live TV to be paused and forwarded has given the consumer control over what he or she consumes.

In fact, technological developments continue to enable users to have more of a say about the world they experience. Products are being designed to allow consumers to call the shots. iPods and music downloads mean that people no longer have to buy a CD for the one decent song that's on an album. Facebook, Twitter and other social networks mean that people can hang out with hundreds of 'friends' around the world, sharing information and gossip. YouTube allows people to see whatever they want, when they want, from around the world. South African TV stations don't screen the programme you want? No problem, you can see it anyway. Maybe it'll become so popular that it'll trigger our TV execs to buy it eventually.

It's all about control, and the people have it.

Every person is an advertising medium, a news channel, an expert. People have always wanted to have their say, and now they have the technology to do so. Joe Average can become an entertainment reporter and a politician can have his career ruined because someone in cyberspace doesn't like him.

People want experiences, not adverts

There's another change taking place among the average consumer. With the world at our fingertips, experiences are becoming more

Pick 'n mix identity

Milisuthando Bongela

It used to be that news was reported and packaged by journalists, designers designed designer shoes, chefs concocted dishes and TV stations controlled television viewing. Today you can select the stories you'd like to read from a screen that gives you options and print your own magazine, you can walk into a store and design your own shoes, go to a restaurant and choose the ingredients for your own dish to be prepared by a chef, and PVR allows you to choose the TV shows you want to watch when you want to watch them.

The formation of identity is no longer based purely on nature and nurture. Just as we can choose what music we like to listen to, we have the freedom to construct an individual identity informed by myriad influences, environments and options. A ten year old in 2010 will have probably never heard the expression 'curiosity killed the cat' because this generation has experienced media, technology and a constitutional and ideological discourse that encourages curiosity, exploration and sampling of as many things on offer as possible.

The most literal representation of how we construct our identities is through the social networking media of Facebook, MXit, MySpace and, most recently, Twitter. We pick and mix how we want the world to see us by constructing our identities using these tools, creating a distorted sense of communication and, ironically, thinking that we are more in touch with each other.

But on the flipside, we are in touch with information that we can use to inform our multi-dimensional identities. We can choose our religion, diet, sexual orientation, cultural practices, career and whether to raise a child in a nuclear, single or same sex-parent environment. Popularised by celebrities such as Brangelina and Madonna, pick and mix families are changing the way we see the family structure.

We use our adornments, be they clothes, cars or ringtones as adjectives to describe our multi-dimensional selves, and it's becoming more difficult to typecast people – a marketer's nightmare. Until now marketers have gotten away with pigeonholing people based on information about their demographic and Living Standards Measure (LSM). This way of categorising stands to become less relevant as people's fluid

TREND SNACK

Pick 'n mix identity *continued*

priorities and choices influence the ways in which they spend their money – making their habits less predictable.

Because we are overwhelmed with choices and unlimited access to information, we tend to pick and mix different things in order to filter and control what we consume to suit our individual needs. Privileged people, who are at the core of this trend, will continue to pick and mix their lifestyles in an attempt to assert their individuality, a trademark of a 21st century mentality.

T R E N D   S N A C K

important. People are seeking something, something meaningful, experiences that connect them with life and with each other.

Even death is no reason to stop searching for those meaningful experiences. A recent *Vanity Fair* article by James Wolcott entitled 'Final-Exit Strategies' ponders the American phenomenon of using death as the ultimate motivation tool.[1] Spearheaded by the book *Tuesdays with Morrie*, fed by the similarly themed *The Last Lecture* and *The Bucket List* to name a few, and with encouragement from Oprah, the message seems to be: experience everything you can as fast as you can, and don't think that lying on your deathbed trying to slip off the mortal coil counts as an excuse.

In this world of connectedness, global interaction like never before and larger-than-life experiences that are shared in the blink of an eye, the traditional advert resembles a black and white, soundless motion picture trying to compete with today's Hollywood blockbusters. Advertising competes in a world of YouTube,

Hollywood star power, social networking sites and the iPod. There's a lot of competition for that tiny spark of interest from the average consumer and its flashy and shiny competitor.

The good news is that the advertising world is starting to get it. Just look at all the recent advertising awards competitions; conventional advertising hardly wins any more. What matters in awards is who Googles it, who passes it on and has it been seen on YouTube. After all, that's where our markets live. Can a campaign really be considered successful if it doesn't rate on page impressions, Twitter posts, Flickr comments and YouTube hits? Consumers are our modern-day PR executives. They pass on information, entertainment and gossip, but only if it interests them. Perhaps, in time, we will see blogs and Twitter groups featured in advertising awards. After all, they are as much a medium as TV, radio and print.

But what makes a piece of communication worthy of being passed on? The marketing world has always considered word of mouth as the gold standard of communication, but tapping into it has always been a hit or miss affair. Now it's 'word of mouse' but still no easier to predict and control. Adverts need to capture the imagination and inspire interaction. They need to be something worth talking about.

The Cadbury's Gorilla ad launched on South African TV in early 2009 but was originally launched internationally online. Through word-of-mouse- and consumer-driven PR, it captured imaginations and became a worldwide phenomenon.[2]

Football's homage to the 'Sistine Chapel' in Cologne has been seen by a handful of people at the station when compared to the millions who have viewed it online.[3]

And in South Africa, there's Highveld Radio, which seems to have perfected the way it interacts with the community. For the most part, the competitions and promotions that the station devises together with its clients have one thing in common – heavy interaction with the consumer. One example of a successful campaign is 'The Fugitive', an annual promotion run on behalf of a client. For the duration of the hunt for Fugi, Johannesburg practically comes to a standstill as everyone gets involved in tracking down this elusive character. Listeners visit the website, join in, read the blog and share information on where Fugi may be found. The reward is cash for the person who eventually finds him, publicity for the client and the creation of a loyal and intimately involved community for the radio station.

And involvement and loyalty definitely go hand in hand. If consumers feel that their product is relevant to their life, that it is designed for their enjoyment and that it is interacting with them, they will be more willing to interact with it. If you compare experiences like that to the experience of a traditional advert, your 30-second shplurb and a pack shot doesn't come up looking too shiny.

The line has blurred between advertising and PR

In some parts of the world, and increasingly in South Africa, it's getting harder and harder to determine where advertising begins and PR ends. As recently as ten years ago, the roles were well-defined – advertising was radio, TV, print and billboard, while PR was internal, reputation management and perhaps a quick ten-liner published in a media magazine about the latest advert. These days, adverts must have a PR element to make a splash.

It seems ironic to quote someone as ancient as Confucius to

make a point about modern advertising, but he got it right when he said: 'Tell me and I will forget. Show me and I may remember. Involve me and I will understand.' I guess modern marketing needs to resort to old-fashioned values of communication.

So what exactly does this mean for advertising? Actually it's good news. Creating something new is always good news.

For a start, advertising can no longer be the thing that interrupts what consumers are interested in, it must be what consumers are interested in. Advertising people need to be entertainers. No one wants to watch an advert, but they do want to watch what is interesting to them. In order to do that, all the old rules need to go out the window. In the past, brand custodians worked out a brief, decided what the benefits of the brand were and then made sure that any advert that followed talked to the benefits. Not to be rude but, who cares? Certainly not the consumer.

People don't crave information in the same way any more, they crave interaction. Cadbury's Gorilla says very little about the chocolate, but you get the idea. Cadbury's comes across as being about joy and, more importantly, as the kind of brand that can be quirky and interesting.

Even the traditional rules on media placement can be rethought. Instead of creating a TV advert and then spending millions ensuring that your ad appears in as many places as your budget will allow, create an experience. Give it 'talkability' and your audience will choose your media for you.

But, of course, people won't pass just anything on; it has to be authentic, and surprising. It has to go back to the idea of creating an experience.

Throwing out the rules also means that we need to find a new way of judging great advertising. We need a new operating system.

We need to ignore what has been done before and follow the example of the world – react faster, create better and get it out there before people move on to the next interesting experience.

Jean-Marie Dru of TBWA once wrote that great brands are powerful only if they take action: 'Great brands are not nouns, but verbs. Apple liberates, IBM solves, Nike exhorts, Virgin challenges, Sony dreams.'[4]

But brands also need to take action in how they communicate. They can't passively tell a consumer what they are selling, they have to actively show and involve. Modern consumers won't abide being talked at, because they don't have to. They live in a world that interacts with them, and that communicates with them. Brands must do the same or run the risk of becoming obsolete and ignored.

In the future, advertising needs to stop being a choice between a print advert or a TV advert or a promotion or an event. Advertising executives need to understand that unless the consumer can feel, taste and experience it, it's on its way out. That doesn't mean we must wave goodbye to the traditional TV advert or send the trusted print advert the way of Betamax; they still have a place, but that place is becoming less exalted. Now they must work harder to win share of mind.

If General Motors were to reinvent itself, what would it do?

At the beginning of 2009, the world reeled when a number of big, seemingly dependable companies filed for bankruptcy on the back of one of the worst economic disasters in decades. Among them

Brand sluts

Sarah Badat

The logo queens of the 1980s and 90s who worshipped Polo ponies and interlocked Chanel Cs have become an endangered species morphing, in line with the principles of evolution, into brand sluts who unapologetically switch brands like sexual partners: easy come, easy go.

Looking at the decline of long-term personal relationships in a society fraught with divorce and infidelity it comes as no surprise that consumers are applying the same promiscuous behaviour to the way they shop. Our obsession with acquisitions and newness has inspired this new breed of licentious shoppers to try out multiple product options before deciding on one and to then move along swiftly when they spot a better deal.

With the vast multitude of brands on offer today, the old notion of being in a long-term monogamous relationship with one brand has all but vanished. According to a study conducted in the USA by Catalina Marketing Corp's Pointer Media Network, just four out of ten brands held on to at least half of their highly loyal customers from 2007 to 2008. The study showed that 48% of highly loyal

consumers stayed that way during the study period, while 19% reduced their loyalty and 33% completely defected to other brands – not exhibiting any brand loyalty at all. When asked if brand loyalty could experience a further decline from 2008 to 2009, Catalina Marketing Vice-President Tod Morris maintained, 'It likely could.'

Consumers today are savvier. They do their homework before making a commitment and are unapologetic about flitting from one brand to the next. The changing nature of shopping and reviewing brand and product offerings online has led to a loss of brand fidelity among consumers who are weary of listening to constant brand noise. We have an office joke about consumers who are starting to demand 'recession packages' rooted in the phenomenon that the economic downturn has induced a culture of astute shoppers who are constantly on the lookout for a better offer.

Marian Salzman, Executive Vice-President of USA-based advertising agency JWT highlights commoditisation, rapid innovation and brand inflation as the driving forces behind brand infidelity. Writing in the *Ivey Business*

Brand sluts *continued*

Journal, international brand expert Jean-Noël Kapferer explains, 'Brand loyalty can no longer exist because the intrinsic nature of the definition of the term is contradictory to the actual relationship between the producer and consumer. Brand loyalty implies a type of matrimonial relationship based on exclusivity and this relationship is impossible because the producer does not reciprocate the relationship.'

For the brand sluts brand loyalty is being replaced with 'brand trust', which is earned when brands live up to their promises and deliver real meaning and satisfaction to their users through product performance and service delivery. Apple is one brand that seems to be enjoying a degree of brand trust in the recession with 56% of iPhone users upgrading to the iPhone 3GS as soon as it was released in the USA earlier this year. This example illustrates that to convert brand sluts into brand evangelists, marketers need to talk to tribes of like-minded consumers instead of using the dwindling mass-market approach. Make them feel included and appreciated and even the most wanton consumers will see the benefits of going steady.

T R E N D   S N A C K

was the 100-year-old stalwart General Motors. How could this happen, we wondered? How could a brand, as much a part of our consciousness as this one is, flounder after thriving for 100 years? Well it has. And now it is working to restore some form of economic viability along with its reputation.

But imagine, for a second, that it was starting out fresh, with no preconceived ideas about how a brand should be built and communicated. If it looked at the world as it is now, not how it has always been, how would it choose to interact with it? Would it create brands that were as flexible as the world is, like iChange, the concept car from Swiss auto powerhouse Rinspeed that changes size depending on how many people are in it?[5] Would it rethink its advertising and selling approach, ignoring traditional mediums for a more modern approach? And, if it did so, would it build its brand faster than in the past? I say yes.

There are industries where learning from past experiences is beneficial, but when building a brand, doing it how it's always been done leaves you playing catch up with your target market.

The rise of people brands

As the sun sets on Hollywood, the rich and famous come out to play. It's the opening of a hot new nightclub – three stories of dance floors, the hottest DJs that money can buy and the promise of a little stargazing. The paparazzi shove elbows with fans as they wait to see who will show up. It's rumoured that Paris will be here. And Britney. It's a safe bet they will be, or they won't get their appearance fee.

According to rumours, Paris Hilton makes between US$37 500 and US$150 000 per appearance. She may be an heiress but being famous costs money and she funds her fame, in large part, through these appearances. Hilton may be the most visible but she certainly isn't the only person famous for being famous. While more traditional stars did something worthy and then got famous, Paris Hilton got famous first and then looked around for something to do.

People brands are a relatively new phenomenon. Yes, there have always been celebrities and they have always marketed themselves to some degree. But there's been a subtle change. It used to be that companies like Nike and Coca-Cola hired celebs to advertise their brands; now celebs are the brands, launching clothing lines, shoe lines, perfumes, anything that they can realistically claim to have authority over. When people buy Paris Hilton's new perfume, they are buying a brand, and that brand just happens to be a person.

Just as technology allows the average consumer more control over what he or she sees and experiences, it also allows the celebrity to have a little more say in how his or her celebrity is managed. And many are choosing to be more accessible.

Surprisingly enough, they are normal human beings and want what most people want – to make a connection and to interact meaningfully. Hop onto Twitter and Facebook and you may be able to hear Lindsay Lohan's thoughts on her romance, or Britney's latest news, or even what Ashton Kutcher thinks of Susan Boyle. In fact, it was Kutcher gushing about Boyle on Twitter that got the world truly hooked on this less than glam Scottish songstress. After only one performance on *Britain's Got Talent* in early 2009, her name flew around the world, she got over 100 million hits on YouTube,[6] and if she launched a throat lozenge, it would probably would have done well too.

The fact is, almost anyone can become a brand. Because a brand no longer has to offer a tangible benefit, an emotional one will do. Create an experience and you'll create a brand. Give people something to write home about, or rather Twitter about, and you can become famous.

The ABC of VIPs

So what does advertising have to learn from these people brands? For a start, they are the perfect example of how brands are being created now, versus how they used to be. People brands don't advertise themselves. Their fame and popularity comes through PR, through interacting with the people they want to attract. And think of the speed with which these brands are being created. Think how difficult it would be for a traditional brand to be worth US$100 million in a year. The speed of the current media landscape means you can build a brand in a few months if you are giving the public what they want.

The second thing we can learn is to give people what they want. People brands are pandering to the public. They are providing content that is interesting and then they are allowing the public to interact with them, and share the experience. People brands fit into our world, not the other way round. When a traditional brand acts in this way, it too will capture the public's imagination. Google, Facebook, Twitter, all grew up very fast. One minute we had hardly heard of them, the next they were an integral part of our lifestyle. They gave us what we wanted, how we wanted it, when we wanted it. They never advertised, and most people probably can't even remember how they heard about these brands or from where, but they arrived in our lives and we embraced them because they became what we want them to be. In fact, if Google and Facebook did advertise they might intrinsically damage their brand. Because they are brands for the people, they are about doing what the consumers want, not telling them what they should be thinking.

Finally, we advertising folk need to learn how to be nimble. Like Britney who regularly reinvents herself, we need to reinvent how we do what we do. The world is changing at a phenomenal rate, and as brand champions we shouldn't just be keeping up, we should be lapping the changes. Instead, many of us are falling behind. The way we do business in the future needs to reflect how the world and our consumers are doing life – being involved, staying connected and seeking out meaningful experiences.

Notes

1 James Wolcott, 'Final-Exit Strategies'. *Vanity Fair*, March 2009.

2 The advert shows a gorilla playing the drums to a Phil Collins song. It can be viewed at www.youtube.com/watch?v=TnzFRV1Lwlo (accessed 30 June 2009).

3 The fresco can be viewed at www.vrmag.org/issue26/ADIDAS_SCORES_WITH_ FIFA_WORLD_CUP_FEVER_FRESCO_IN_COLOGNE.html (accessed 30 June 2009).

4 Jean-Marie Dru, www.mad-blog.com/category/top_stories (accessed 30 June 2009).

5 Read more about Rinspeed's iChange at www.rinspeed.com/pages/cars/ ichange/pre-ichange.htm (accessed 30 June 2009).

6 To see Susan Boyle's performance on *Britain's Got Talent*, go to www.youtube. com/watch?v=9lp0IWv8QZY (accessed 30 June 2009).

Recession and the war for talent

Is the war for talent over?

Italia Boninelli

Italia Boninelli's interest in talent management and skills pipelines arose out of a realisation that traditional Human Resources (HR) approaches to strategic skills shortages in South Africa were woefully inadequate. Boninelli has headed up HR functions in banking, healthcare and mining, and is now Senior Vice-President, Human Resources at mining company Gold Fields. She entered the industry at a time when the company faced tremendous challenges around cost containment, high labour turnover, international expansion and archaic HR systems. She evolved the HR function beyond administratively focused delivery, introducing an HR Shared Services Centre while simultaneously developing HR practitioners to be able to apply business knowledge at Gold Fields.

Her commitment to uplifting skills in the profession has seen her lecture at business schools and for professional bodies. Some of her findings have been published in two books used as university set works, *Building Human Capital* and *Conversations in Leadership: South African Perspectives*.

A founder member of the National Human Resources Research Initiative of the South African Board for Personnel Practice – setting the research agenda of strategic HR practices – Boninelli has received much recognition in her field and was awarded 'HR Director of 2008' by the Institute for People Management of South Africa.

She is a registered industrial psychologist with a Master's degree in Psychology from the University of the Witwatersrand and a post-graduate diploma in labour relations from the University of South Africa (UNISA).

THE STRATEGIC management of Human Resources (HR) always occurs within a broader socio-political and business context. This will be no less true for the war for talent in South Africa in 2010 and beyond.

In a recent FutureWorld survey of 37 countries,[1] the top issues keeping global executives awake at night relate to concerns around the global economic slowdown. This was followed closely by staffing and skills. In joint third place were resource management (raw materials, fuel costs and electricity) and profitability, followed by concerns about business performance (increased competition, efficiencies and productivity).

It should come as no surprise that concerns about staffing and skills ranked first by some margin as the issue keeping South African executives up at night.

The war for talent

The skills shortage in South Africa is a topic that has provoked much heated debate in recent years and enjoyed extensive media coverage. Some argue it is a pressing concern while others say it is the stuff of urban legend (for example, Jimmy Manyi).[2]

The debate is far from over. According to consultancy firm Grant Thornton's *International Business Report 2009*, 41% of South Africa's privately held businesses cite the lack of availability of a skilled workforce as the biggest constraint to business growth.[3] Ernst & Young, one of the world's leading professional services organisations, comments:

> In South Africa, the biggest contributor to mining skills short-
> ages [is] HIV/AIDS, followed by the emigration of experienced
> and skilled workers. In the past 40 years it is estimated a third
> of South Africa's engineering graduates have emigrated.
> South Africa also has a legacy of poor education for 90% of
> the population.[4]

Much has been written about the crisis in South African education and one only has to look at a few key statistics to understand that the situation is far from ideal. Only 4% of matriculants have higher grade mathematics, and 65% of these come from just 7% of the schools.[5] The number of artisans tested across all trades has dropped from 26 500 in 1986 to 9 041 in 2008. The average age of an artisan in South Africa today is between 53 and 56 meaning that most will retire within ten years.[6] A Human Sciences Research Council study showed that 60% of enrolled students drop out of university. Of the 304 240 people who enrolled for engineering degrees between 1998 and 2006, only 11.75% graduated.[7] South Africa, relative to its development levels, is already lagging behind other countries. Data from the Federation of Engineering Contractors shows South Africa has 1 engineer for every 3 200 people, compared with 1 in 150 in India, 1 in 250 in Europe and 1 in every 400–450 for Australia and the USA.[8] Many in government, trade unions and the business community have pinned their hopes on an investment of ever-increasing amounts of resources deployed to solve the problems in the education system to rectify the skills shortage. The failure of the recapitalised Further Education and Training colleges in late 2007 – where pass rates ranged from 11–20% because the students had been merely processed rather than screened for their ability to understand the subject matter – is proof to the contrary. There is also growing recognition that the Sector Education and Training Authorities (SETAs) were guilty of underspending to the tune of R4 billion as of late 2007, and have not been delivering.[9] Figures show that 81% of the learners who register with SETAs do not complete their training courses.

You don't have to look far to find tangible evidence of a growing workforce *experience gap*. The reason often depends on the industry. Some companies are facing shortages largely because of demand increases. But usually it is a combination of factors, such as power utilities that have seen demand grow and technology skills increase, and have a large portion of their workforce eligible for retirement (in many critical jobs as many as half of the workforce) with few experienced workers in their 30s and 40s left behind to do the work.[10]

At the same time, those who are talented, with good qualifications and skills, have been in high demand. This has resulted in the acceleration of career cycles and pay due to the shortage of skills and the pressure to reach affirmative action targets.

This fast rise up the career ladder for relatively young and inexperienced people has seen many being placed in senior positions without ever having faced tough decisions, and carried mainly by their energy, enthusiasm and creativity. They have often skipped out on building real depth to go straight into management positions but as many have discovered, this 'experience gap' is not so easily bridged.

I have coached or mentored many senior managers and executives who feel inadequate to deal with the demands of their jobs, but cannot openly admit to feeling this way. Instead, the constant knocking on their door of headhunters has provided them with the escape hatch to the next job before the chickens come home to roost.

For those with both skills and experience, there have been no limits as to what they could demand in remuneration and benefits. The previous long cycle of economic boom and unprecedented growth has meant for almost everyone in the workforce, but particularly for those with key skills, a period of prosperity, good jobs, easy promotions and salary increases.

In short, before this global recession it was said that 'globally employers have been forced to recognise that the war for talent is over, and talent has won'.[11]

The global economic recession

The first impact of the current global economic crisis has been on the expectations of employees. One of the features of this recession is that there are 'those too young to remember anything other than a buoyant global economy with unprecedented opportunities for education and employment, and being wooed and fought over by glossy corporate recruiting teams'.[12] They may never have contemplated being made redundant so early in their careers. Prosperity has left many employees with unrealistic expectations about what our daily efforts should bring.

Alain de Botton, philosopher and author of *The Pleasures and Sorrows of Work*, writes:

> *In an economic crisis, the gloves come off and power is more cleanly revealed again. So one of the benefits of the crisis is that it enables us to lower our expectations as to what work can deliver. Some of the greater existential questions disappear. Simply holding down an ordinary job and surviving comes to seem like reward enough.*[13]

Even though South Africa seems to have taken less of a hit relative to the rest of the world in this crisis, the psychological impact on employees has been noticeable. We are entering a period of austerity with people rethinking what is important to them. Employees are starting to think about their previous ambitions and whether they are realistic in this kind of economic downturn. As a result, the attraction and retention pressures on most companies will become less intense and poaching activity should decrease.

We may experience a temporary respite in the talent war. Companies are restructuring and downsizing and there is a short-term increase in people available in the market compared to what has been the case in recent years (but not necessarily in key skills). Voluntary turnover is dropping as people stay put in an insecure job market where 'last in, first out' may see you on the retrenchment list. Smaller companies going under or bigger companies retrenching have seen skilled staff and even executives being prepared to take jobs they would not normally accept and to work for less.

However, it is likely that as soon as the economy turns and employment markets open up again these individuals will move on very quickly. Another feature has been the forced early retirement of more expensive but more experienced senior managers and executives for cost-saving reasons, leaving the young talent in the organisation relatively exposed, without mentors and without the organisational memory that assisted decision-making in difficult times.

There is a widespread freeze on recruitment and protectionism is creeping into the international market. There have been increased restrictions on work permits for foreign workers with governments imposing limits on the number of expatriate multinationals that may be hired as they try to ensure jobs for their own citizens. This may result in expatriate South Africans returning from overseas postings to their home country as their conditions of employment become too expensive for companies and foreign job opportunities become more limited. For the same reasons, less of our key skills are likely to be emigrating in the next few years.

While many companies have been forced to implement reduced increases and low or no bonuses as a result of the economic recession, it must be remembered that with few incentives and underwater shares the 'golden handcuffs' are gone and this may still pose a threat to the retention of key skills even in the current market. Top talent may look for the safest port in a storm and move to industries that are relatively less affected by the crisis.

Another emerging trend is that older employees are finding that their retirement savings are seriously underfunded. As a result, 'near retirees' are asking to stay on and many retirees are returning to work full-time or part-time to supplement their retirement income. This is an opportunity to utilise experience and skills, not simply to fill vacancies and solve short-term problems, but also to mentor and train youngsters in the pipeline. In the engineering professions, for example, a key issue is the lack of experienced professionals to mentor new graduates, which is widely attributed to an exodus of experienced skills from the country. This has a major impact on the transfer of skills, many of which can only be acquired tacitly and on the job from experienced mentors.

In times of economic crisis, one of the first areas to be cut in most companies is the training budget. This recession is no exception. In an informal survey conducted recently of major companies across several industries in South Africa, many were considering cuts in training budgets. We have not learnt from previous cycles where the knee-jerk reaction of cutting training budgets in hard times drastically reduced graduate and technical pipelines, leaving very little capacity for the upswing when it inevitably occurred.

The companies that will win in the long run are those that are prepared to make the investment in their staff even in the hard times because they understand that simply to maintain the status quo of skills (and without providing for the drain caused by emigration, HIV/AIDS, and impending retirements) will require a huge challenge to recruit, develop and retain the right quality, number and committed skills.

In the current economic crisis, companies in many countries can take the opportunity in the slowdown to assess their organisations, think through their workforce strategies and structures, and make strategic adjustments while the environment is changed. There is an urgent need to review the current composition and capabilities of the workforce, determine the short- and long-term workforce needs, and make more informed decisions about the talent needed to survive and eventually thrive.

This is also a good time for companies to bring in some key talent that was not accessible in the past. To do this, companies need to ensure that they can articulate a career path and opportunities for their employees, so that these same employees are not hopping to the next job as soon as the economy turns if they don't receive quick promotions and salary increases.

How has HR dealt with the crisis?

The challenges to HR professionals are that not only are many still lacking the data, tools and processes they need to be effective, but the bigger challenge relates to their skill-sets, mindsets and capabilities. A lot of HR teams in the past were caught up in transactional and administrative activities and were unable to act as change agents and business partners in terms of leadership development, organisational development and enterprise transformation. Business leaders have been saying that HR teams often lack business acumen and a real understanding of the business, which has meant that they lack credibility with the line and are ineffective in coaching their business leaders in terms of how to manage the war for talent effectively.

If they have not already done so, HR teams need to utilise technology and process re-engineering to manage and deliver existing HR services more efficiently. This will relieve them of the volume of transactional activities (repetitive activities that could be done by lower-level administrative staff, such as answering queries on HR policies and the administration of leave and employee moves), freeing them up to create new tiered HR structures as follows:

❑ HR service centres that provide first-line communication with all employees and first-line managers;
❑ Centres of expertise with content experts who design common solutions applied across organisational boundaries; and
❑ HR business partners who are assigned to work with specific business units to ensure that business strategies are supported with 'best fit' HR interventions.

This will assist in creating the capacity to address the most pressing priority for HR – ensuring the pipeline of skills. A pipeline of the right number and quality of skilled talent is a function of several things:

❑ *Number of people with the required qualifications:* This relates to turnover, vacancy factors and supply in the marketplace. There is an urgent need to review current composition and capabilities of the workforce, determine the short- and long-term workforce needs and make more informed decisions about the talent needed to survive and, eventually, thrive;

❏ *Competence levels:* The mere presence of a qualification does not in any way guarantee competence. The declining standards and shortage of qualified teaching staff in many educational institutions has meant that many graduates or diplomates come with some degree of skills gap. In addition, a qualification may be the starting point for true competence as success in a role may require knowledge of many other things. Existing internal skills need to be identified and assessed to determine competency levels and potential for ongoing training and development;

❏ *Utilisation of skills:* Often skills are inappropriately utilised in the workplace. In a study conducted in a healthcare company I previously worked for, we established that professional nursing staff were spending less than 43% of their time on activities that actually required a nursing qualification.[14] This reinforces the need for companies to look carefully at productivity and review how jobs are designed and resourced. In cases of severe skills shortage, it may require a re-engineering of the workplace to get away with less of the high-level skills;

❏ *Performance management:* Performance objectives have to be closely aligned to the strategy of the company. It has been said what gets measured gets done and what gets paid for gets done more. The linkage between performance and pay should have a direct impact on productivity. But HR will have to take another look at remuneration strategy in the current economic crisis. The key issue for employers today is how to get the best out of their people by understanding the real employee value proposition. A Conference Board study (reported by Deloitte) asked employees what they expected from their employers.[15] The top three responses were: interesting, challenging work; open, two-way communication; and, opportunities for growth and development. And money? It finished eighth. People are motivated not only by financial rewards but by challenge, professional growth, recognition and development opportunities, among other factors. Understanding how to package this becomes key for employee retention; and

❏ *Employee engagement:* Nothing can replace the personal commitment of employees and their willingness to go the extra mile. Most companies strive to 'maximise shareholder wealth' – a goal that is inadequate in many respects. As an emotional catalyst, wealth maximisation lacks the power to mobilise fully human energies. It is an insufficient defence when people question the legitimacy of corporate power. And it is particularly true in an economic recession when retrenchments and other cost-cutting inevitably results in poor employee morale and anxiety around job security.

So is the war for talent over?

The expectation may well be that with the global economic recession and widespread layoffs, more skills will be available and surely skills shortages are a thing of the past. The reality is that despite the troubled economy and the resulting need for companies to cut expenses, there is still a significant shortage of talent. There is going to be another round in the war for talent, but unlike previous boom times when employees were driving title and compensation inflation – this will be a new game with new rules.

A breakdown in trust has sown the seeds of a management crisis as the massive egos, excessive bonuses and highly individualistic approaches taken by senior line managers and executives during the good times are seen as being partly responsible for today's problems. Shareholders have been outraged and the international press has widely publicised inappropriate executive pay. Governments are imposing greater governance around remuneration and other staffing practices.

The Group of Twenty (G-20) and the Financial Stability Forum (FSF) are both examining remuneration issues to ensure effective governance and oversight of executive remuneration as part of their responses to the crisis. The UK and the USA have imposed conditions on remuneration for entities that have received the benefit of recent corporate bailouts and government assistance packages. The German government and the Australian government have imposed tough new rules governing executive pay. The changes to the Companies Act in South Africa together with the governance implications of King III[16] will augur in a new era of transparency and accountability in remuneration and other staffing practices. These changes will see increased personal accountability of directors and executives. For example, the new Companies Act in South Africa allows not only shareholders but also employees to bring derivative actions against delinquent board directors and/or executive management.

South Africa also does not operate in isolation from the rest of the world. The economic recession won't provide the relief this time around that might be expected because of the economic stimulus plans that the central and local governments in the USA, UK and China have put together. It is expected that when the stimulus packages kick in, the global economy is likely to start recovering again.

Most companies will then continue to battle for a limited amount of resources in the international labour market, often to lose against those with deeper financial pockets or be forced to pay too much. Building a technical or leadership pipeline can take years of careful cultivation and a significant investment of time and money.

Leadership in recession

In turbulent times we look to organisations that share our concerns, manage anxiety and take the lead. In these difficult times of economic crisis, leaders play a central role in not only attracting new talent but also in retaining and motivating the remaining talent within an organisation. Leaders must step up and take a proactive role in addressing workforce concerns while simultaneously tending to the demands of the external market. But after years of growth, many managers have no experience of a recession. They are also ill-equipped to deal with the crisis as historically management development programmes were too focused on technical skills and old-fashioned managerial skills (planning, organising, delegating, and controlling) as opposed to building the broader business acumen and leadership skills needed.

According to a Deloitte study, the number one reason that people leave their jobs is due to their relationship with their boss.[17] Organisations may therefore want to kick off their talent management strategies by first examining the deployment and development of the people tasked with leading others.

Conclusion

There is no doubt that without the right skills in place, you can't execute your business plan. Even the most well-crafted business strategy has little value unless it can be implemented successfully by a qualified workforce. In the past, during times of consolidation, businesses could afford to take a shorter-term outlook on determining workforce requirements, buying talent as needed. However, today we see many industries retrenching workers in certain categories while still actively recruiting in others because they have more highly technically skilled and managerial jobs than qualified workers. With the uncertainty of the markets and the fluidity of new trends emerging in the war for talent, executives and HR practitioners alike will continue to face significant challenges in ensuring that the organisation has the experienced, highly skilled talent it needs to survive and to thrive.

Notes

1 FutureWorld Flash Survey, 'What's Keeping Executives Awake at Night?' FutureWorld, 2008, www.futureworld.co.za/Public Zone/Survey2008 (accessed 30 June 2009).

2 Centre for Development and Enterprise Report, 'Six Myths about South Africa's Skills Shortage', 1 March 2007. Mzwanele 'Jimmy' Manyi is Chairperson for the Commission for Employment Equity and Deputy President of the Black Management Forum. His views have been widely reported by the media.

3 Grant Thornton International Ltd, 'International Business Report 2009'. See www.grantthorntonibos.com (accessed 30 June 2009).

4 Charlotte Matthews, 'Mining Industry Needs to Get Smart on Skills'. *Business Day*, 30 April 2009.

5 Sarah Howie, 'Third International Mathematics and Science Study Repeat (TIMSS-R)', HSRC Press; 1998/DoE Teachers for the Future 2005: Meeting Teacher Shortages to Achieve Education for All Pretoria; DoE; 2005, 46–47.

6   Prakash Naidoo, 'Skills. Mind the Gap'. *Financial Mail*, 9 December 2008.

7   *HSRC Student Pathway Study* (HSRC Press, 2008).

8   Sanchia Temkin, 'Russia can Help Ease SA Skills Crisis'. *Business Day*, 5 December 2007.

9   Sue Blaine, 'SETAs Defend their R 3.7bn Cash Pile'. *Business Day*, 1 November 2007.

10 Jay Doherty, 'Reducing Business Risk through Effective Workforce Planning'. *Human Capital Perspective*, Volume 3, Issue 1, 2009.

11 Sandra Burmeister, 'Mining Industry Responds to Skills Development Challenge'. Consulting Web, 24 July 2008, www.consultingweb.co.za/index2 (accessed 30 June 2009).

12 Janet Davies, 'Redundancy: Is it Really the End?' *Hourglass*, Issue 13, March 2009.

13 Alain de Botton, *The Pleasures and Sorrows of Work* (Hamish Hamilton, 2009).

14 Italia Boninelli and Adele Thomas, 'Appropriate Skills Utilisation, South African Board for Personnel Practice Case Study 2009/10', April 2009.

15 Deloitte Research Report, 'It's 2008: Do you Know Where your Talent is? Connecting People to what Matters', 5 June 2008.

16 Rob Rose, 'The Next King Corporate Governance Code'. *Financial Mail*, 20 July 2007. King III is a Draft Report for Corporate Governance for South Africa that was released for comment on 25 February 2009. See www.iodsa.co.za (accessed 30 June 2009).

17 Deloitte Research Report, 5 June 2008.

FLUX OBSERVATION

The career revolution

Carina Louw

THE GLOBAL economic crisis has resulted in a reassessment of career paths as thousands of jobs are being wiped out. As workers have to confront the reality of mass retrenchments, some have embraced this possibility as an opportunity to reshape their working lives.

For these workers there is not a lot to lose by taking a risk and pursuing a new direction. There is, instead, a lot to be gained by taking control of the uncertainty and custom-designing their own career. Moreover, it is easier than ever to work remotely and outside of regular business hours, signalling the decline of the nine-to-five work week.

We are approaching a tipping point in which a growing number of people will be moving away from traditional employment towards careers that will comprise multiple freelance or part-time jobs and be characterised by increasing mobility and flexibility.

Makeshift careers

Freelancing is not new to the writers, photographers, designers, musicians and other creative workers who have been doing it for years. What is changing now is that as the economy worsens more high-income professionals in fields previously known for their rigidity, such as finance, law and human resources, are starting to freelance.

Employers are waking up to the notion that flexibility makes economic sense and are turning to freelancers as a way to reduce their personnel costs. Companies are increasingly hiring specialists in specific areas who can come in and consult, or do project work. According to statistics two-thirds of the opportunities created in 2008 in the UK were part-time, temporary or contract-based.

Employees are voluntarily choosing a three- or four-day working week, or finding other ways to reduce their time at work. Job sharing, wherein two or more people share one full-time job by dividing the time and paycheque, is becoming increasingly popular as a means to help employers avoid mass layoffs. With more free time on their hands these job sharers are now pursuing a second career or multiple vocations simultaneously. Online education is exploding as bankers, conveyancers and other professionals set out to learn new skills. Many professionals, whose first job came after years and years of studying for a degree, are adding other radically different skills to their résumés, such as massage therapy, interior decorating, or other kinds of certificate courses.

People are now starting to custom-blend careers out of multiple part-time jobs that are turning the notion of moonlighting on its head. Whereas moonlighting was often something you did on the sly, working as a lawyer slash yoga instructor or as a doctor slash creative writer, in this day and age it suddenly has cachet.

The concept of having two jobs is not novel. However, there is a more flexible approach to career paths where it is possible to juggle dual roles by having two careers that are not necessarily related, often with one connected to a professional career and the other connected to a side interest or passion. Besides adding multiple income streams, having a dual- or tri-track career enables you to combine your interests and introduce variety. Plus careers accommodating these intersections are often where innovation is born.

The idea of a 'makeshift' career also resonates with the trend towards more individualism. People desire a greater sense of control over their working lives and want to define their own distinctive work style.

Rise of the creative entrepreneurial class

The economic downturn has hit the demographic that used to assume that a university degree from an elite institution was the passport to job security heaven. With the imploding financial and housing sectors a number of people are switching lanes to more creative vocations that they were attracted to but eschewed for the lack of financial security. Now, with the new-born philosophy that there is little to lose, bankers and lawyers are undergoing extreme career makeovers, transforming themselves into cartoonists, stand-up comedians and actors.

New companies, such as the American-based Vocation Vacations, arrange experiential working vacations in a variety of coveted occupations – chocolatier, wedding planner, spa owner, filmmaker – for a week or so in a chosen field. This enables a person to test-drive the career that he or she is interested in without investing time and money in a transition that may turn out to be unsuitable.

There is a huge rise in entrepreneurship as growing numbers of people who have lost their jobs and are rather quickly growing tired of looking for work are creating the job that they want for themselves. Even in tough financial times taking a risk to start the business that you have always dreamt of isn't quite the financial leap of faith it once was.

The Internet has become a relatively easier and low-cost launch pad for start-ups where products or services can instantly compete with big brands on a global scale without betraying a home-based operation. The online world has given people an extraordinary tool to perform all kinds of functions cheaper than it has ever been possible to do before. From interacting with customers, finding business partners and suppliers, to keeping the books can all be done at the click of a button.

In addition, as more and more people have to come up with creative solutions to generate an extra income the world is seeing a boom in the creative and crafts industry. With online markets such as Etsy for buying and selling handmade goods, anyone has the opportunity to turn their hobby into an extra source of income on the side. In fact, some designers, artists and creatives feel liberated from the constraints of their day jobs that only serve to pay the rent and are taking increasing risks to work freelance or sell their work online. There will be an even bigger rise in the creative classes as the younger generation takes over. They'll not only be the first generation to be fully trained in operating in an online world but also the first generation to be completely comfortable with taking on multiple jobs at once.

It's all about values

Our resistance to working fewer hours is more of a cultural issue than an economic one. In contemporary culture high-powered fast-track careers are seen as synonymous with success and it has become the norm to work gruelling hours and to retire late in life.

The accelerated pace of technological development has also meant that instead of working more efficiently most people are just working longer hours in order to finish larger workloads.

The economic crisis is more than an economic slowdown, it is forcing people to slow down and re-evaluate.

New career choices will be driven by values and success will be defined not by title or superiority within a company but by getting what matters to you personally. People no longer want to work ridiculous hours in a soul-diminishing job, and even if they enjoy working in their profession they will want to work less to spend more time with friends and family or doing other things that they enjoy. According to a survey by UK-based company Silver Stork Research, women between the ages of 17 and 28 deemed 'more time' the most important thing that they could give to their children compared with what their parents gave to them. Up to 90% of the women said they would be willing to take a pay cut in order to spend more time with their children. The survey went on to examine how the workforce should change to accommodate these ideals, finding that 78% said flexible work schedules are a necessity and 59% said that establishing better parenting hours, for example a workday that goes from 9 a.m. to 3 p.m., would also be a prerequisite.

Changing workforce

Within ten years the composition of organisations and the structure of the working day will change completely. The working environment in large companies will transform as the online model makes working in ad hoc teams easier and more productive than ever. Every organisation will have to deal with an increasingly complex, restless, age-diverse and highly specialised workforce; from know-it-all 20 year olds to not-quite-ready-to-retire 80 year olds. Outmoded hierarchical management styles will be replaced by leaders who are culturally dexterous on a global scale, who have the ability to find the essential people and outsource jobs to the rest, and who can organise and sustain a network of diverse employees and contacts.

Moreover, the new generation of employees who are now entering the workforce are rejecting the concept of a traditional career. To them, putting in long years of effort at any one company in exchange for a series of raises and promotions is laughable. On top of this, they do not want to work the regular 9 a.m. to 5 p.m. hours because it interferes with their other interests, hobbies and activities.

Organisations that can attract, engage, retain and amuse young talent will be the ones that find success in the rapidly evolving global economy. Companies can no longer treat workers as machines and will increasingly have to adapt to employees' individual needs and formulate new reward and remuneration systems.

Policies that provide for multiple jobs and career paths will be critical if an organisation wants to have any hope of retaining employees for a longer term. In addition, the complete lack of a safety net for freelance workers is one of the crucial challenges that the financial sector will need to address. Banks, insurance and medical aid companies will need to create new services, policies and support structures in order to remain relevant to this new breed of consumer. There will be huge potential for those companies that tap into this largely ignored workforce and provide flexible yet tailor-made loan and insurance packages for individuals with unconventional employment structures.

People's career mindsets are changing as they realise that they don't have to go to work in suits and ties and play the corporate game to be successful. We are witnessing the death of the long-term, one-track career and corporate loyalty, which will soon be but a quaint memory from the previous century. Moreover, a number of social commentators see the move by many away from the financial and housing sectors towards more creative industries as part of a necessary economic recalibration. By inadvertently liberating people from stale jobs and forcing them to think of inventive ways to earn a living, the financial crisis – ironically – has the potential to rejuvenate the metabolism of economies.

According to a recent survey, more than one-quarter of UK workers will not work a conventional work week within the next five years. Predictions are that when the world economy improves, there will be a core group of autonomous workers who won't return to full-time jobs. As a result 2010, may well become known as the year of the career revolution.

References

Jim Carroll, 'Integrating Gen-Y into the Workplace'. Jimcarroll.com, 2008, www.jimcarroll.com/articles/assoc-12.htm (accessed 10 June 2009).

Laura Fitzpatrick, 'We're Getting off the Ladder'. *Time*, 25 May 2009, www.time.com/time/specials/packages/article/0,28804,1898024_1898023_1898076,00.html (accessed 29 May 2009).

Seth Godin, 'The Last Days of Cubicle Life'. *Time*, 25 May 2009, www.time.com/time/specials/packages/article/0,28804,1898024_1898023_1898077,00.html (accessed 29 May 2009).

Professional Contractors Group, 'Study Reveals 1.4 Million Freelancers in the UK: A Significant 14% Growth over the Last Ten Years'. 18 September 2008, www.pcg.org.uk/cms/index.php?option=com_content&view=article&id=4566:study-reveals-14-million-freelancers-in-the-uk-a-significant-14-growth-over-the-last-ten-years&catid=530:press-releases&Itemid=1050 (accessed 5 February 2009).

Josh Quittner, 'The New Internet Start-Up Boom: Get Rich Slow'. *Time*, 9 April 2009, www.time.com/time/magazine/article/0,9171,1890387,00.html (accessed 22 April 2009).

Matt Richtel and Jenna Wortham, 'Weary of Looking for Work, Some Create their Own'. The New York Times Online, 13 March 2009, www.nytimes.com/2009/03/14/technology/start-ups/14startup.html?_r=1&em=&pagewanted=print (accessed 15 June 2009).

FLUX OBSERVATION

Knowledge: The new commodity[1]

Sarah Badat

SWISS BUSINESS school IMD identified the 'changing economics of information and knowledge' as one of the twelve global macro trends that will shape the future.[2] With natural resources becoming scarcer by the day it is no wonder that knowledge production is becoming a global imperative. The rapid pulse of globalisation coupled with the surge of online information is leading to a shift away from a resource-based to a knowledge-based economy that thrives on the production and diffusion of knowledge and information to generate economic wealth.

It is not a new fact that knowledge plays a crucial role in economic development. Economies have always utilised knowledge to perform even the simplest economic activities. What is new, however, is the degree to which knowledge and information are being incorporated into economic activity as commodities. This will have a profound impact on institutions that will be forced to rethink their strategies in an age where 'ideas' – that are subsequently converted into 'knowledge' – are fast gaining a direct exchange value.

The economics of knowledge

The knowledge economy is based on the idea that knowledge has fundamentally different characteristics from physical commodities and therefore the nature of traditional economic activity and our current understanding of it are changing.

Knowledge has unique characteristics. Unlike a physical commodity it cannot be destroyed by consumption. Its value can be enjoyed again and again as new users access it and the return on investment can be significantly higher. While the initial costs of knowledge production (conducting research) can be very high, once it is produced the cost of storing, manipulating and transmitting information is virtually zero and the value of the reproduction of knowledge can be tremendous. The knowledge economy thus places emphasis on the exchange value of ideas.

American organisation TED caught the wave first with its thinking that is modelled on making knowledge and ideas free to the world. TED started out in the 1980s with an annual conference that brings together experts across disciplines to share their ideas with a global community. TED believes in the power of ideas to change lives and, ultimately, the world.

In South Africa we have tended to undervalue ideas and we struggle to measure and define the 'value' of thoughts and concepts as tangible commodities. To participate in the knowledge economy we will have to come up with new ways of packaging and presenting ideas as 'goods' that can be traded as readily as physical commodities.

In June 2009 the London-based Wilkinson Gallery hosted the 'Artwork that Ideas can Buy' project by Italian artist Cesare Pietroiusti.[3] All the exhibited artworks were up for sale but the public could not buy them with cash. Visitors were instead asked to leave proposals, suggestions and opinions related to any artwork in a box, and at the end of the exhibition the comments were opened and the ideas made public. The artist then decided if any of the ideas equated to the value of the artwork and if so, the author of the idea was given the artwork in exchange without paying any money. It's one way of using knowledge as a means of executing economic transactions.

The knowledge economy in practice

The knowledge economy relies on the creation of knowledge through educational and economic initiatives and its dissemination to individuals and corporations across the globe. Firms will have to become centres that facilitate learning, continually adapting management practices and structure to accommodate new technologies and to grasp the emerging opportunities they present. The knowledge economy will see firms banding together to form knowledge networks where interactive learning involving creators, producers and users takes place with the common goal of generating and exchanging information to encourage innovation.

Collaboration plays a starring role in the knowledge economy. Firms will start searching for links with complementary industry players to promote inter-firm knowledge creation. These relationships will help firms to spread the costs and risks associated with innovation, gain access to new research material and share assets in technology, marketing and distribution. As firms experiment with developing new processes, they will determine activities to be undertaken individually or in collaboration with other firms or research institutions.

Don Tapscott, author of *Wikinomics*, highlights the importance of 'peer-to-peer' knowledge-sharing across organisational boundaries to build networks of expertise.[4] He admits that this raises concerns over copyright and intellectual property law in the marketplace but feels strongly that businesses must engage in collaboration to survive.

Hub Culture is a distinctive example of an organisation that generates and shares information through collaborative efforts.[5] The world's first socially operated company comprises over 20 000 members globally. It works to create valuable business opportunities by connecting people through the exchange of knowledge and it even helps drive deals using its digital currency, Ven. The Ven is currently traded at 10 Vens to US$1 and is considered to be the world's first knowledge currency. The website offers a suite of tools to enhance collaboration and content is created by knowledge-rich experts across various disciplines who publish for themselves and the network.

The online community soon manifested itself in the offline world with Hub Culture Pavilions, permanent workspaces for members, sprouting up in urban hubs including London, New York, Hong Kong and Singapore. Organisations like Hub Culture represent a growing movement towards the creation of business networks that knowledge workers can tap into to share and acquire knowledge.

Knowledge workers

Knowledge workers are the foundation on which the knowledge economy is based. They are essentially people who are either 'paid to think' (knowledge producers operating in the field of knowledge production through research) or 'paid to use' (knowledge reproducers operating in the field of knowledge transmission and application). Dr David Abdulai of the Graduate School of Business Leadership at UNISA maintains that knowledge workers do not care for hierarchy.[6] This is because knowledge work is not concerned with traditional social or cultural demographic punctuations of age, race, gender, religion or the physical strength required for industrial labour. What is important is what is in your head and how you can add value to the organisation. From this angle the knowledge economy is a true leveller.

Knowledge workers are different from the traditional workforce where the worker serves the system until the employer decides their skills have become obsolete, which then leads to retrenchment or downsizing. In the knowledge economy the knowledge workers realise that an organisation needs them more than they need employment so they view themselves as essential assets, rather than as subordinates to company owners. This will be difficult to swallow for organisations that cling to past notions of corporate hierarchy, but if these organisations want to remain successful, they will have no choice but to recognise this growing movement.

With knowledge workers outnumbering all other workers in North America by a margin of at least four to one, it has become clear that these workers hold the key to the competitive advantage of organisations. This is because knowledge workers are the source of a company's intangible assets that account for more than half of the worth of most public companies today. According to HR specialist Ann Andrews, in the Knowledge Age only 2% of the workforce will work the land, 10% will work in industry and the remaining 88% will be knowledge workers.

As we enter this new age, the employment policies of firms will increasingly need to be based on the quality-of-life factors that are important to attracting and retaining knowledge workers.

Building human capital

The knowledge economy is heralding the age of human capital. It's not only what you know that is important but also who you are and who is listening to you that contributes to your overall cultural capital. The Internet has made it possible for anyone to have an audience but cultural capital is measured according to the profile of your listeners.

Trend doyenne Li Edelkoort carries cultural capital like a handbag

– effortlessly. Not only does she generate trend knowledge of astounding quality; her listeners are captains of industry from across the globe making her someone worth listening to.

Higher education institutions play a crucial role in developing the human capital necessary to participate effectively in the knowledge economy and their efforts have come under close scrutiny. Writing in *The New York Times*, Mark C. Taylor called graduate education 'the Detroit of higher learning'.[7] According to Taylor, academic programmes produce graduates for which there is no market and develop skills for which there is little demand. He cites the narrow scholarship (research in sub-fields within sub-fields) encouraged by most universities as a tool for creating clones that are unable to navigate the changing economic landscape. The mass-production university model has led to separation between faculties where there should instead be interdisciplinary collaboration, and to ever-increasing specialisation where there should be cross-disciplinary knowledge production. Taylor proposes a complete restructuring of curricula in graduate and undergraduate programmes.

This trend has found currency with the shift in South African higher education institutions towards designing holistic learning programmes that result in cross-field outcomes rather than narrow scholarship as part of the restructuring of the higher education system. However, the pressure towards realising these programmes and the weakening of the traditional course and faculty boundaries remains significantly contested in many of the country's top academic institutions.

For Taylor, academic curricula should be designed to resemble complex networks where students engage in converging branches of learning that encourage the 'beyond-the-box' thinking required by knowledge workers.

As in business, collaboration between educational institutions will become necessary for participation in the knowledge economy. Universities will start to form partnerships to share students and faculty members, making it possible to offer programmes that deliver on higher order critical cross-field outcomes. By preparing students for jobs through new learning approaches and exposure to real-world issues, universities will be able to produce graduates who can easily adapt to a changing economy.

South Africa and the knowledge economy

Through a wide range of initiatives, policy arrangements and collaborations implemented by government departments, South Africa's foundations in the knowledge economy have already been laid. Evidence of this ethos includes the National Qualifications Framework, the close alignment of the Departments of Labour and Education, the SETA structures as well as the Skills Development Act, all of which address critical issues around developing strategies for knowledge production and diffusion.

With the recent split of the Department of Education into separate Ministries, one for Basic Education and the other for Higher Education and Training, government is showing a commitment to reforming higher education, ensuring that academic institutions produce graduates who can compete effectively in the knowledge economy.

As early as 2002, Ben Ngubane, then the Minister of Science and Technology, said in an address on the National Research and Development Strategy: 'Government recognises the key role it plays in providing an enabling environment for innovation and research and in building human capital that we require for the future knowledge economy.' It will take decades to develop the South African workforce into effective knowledge workers but the government is taking a realistic approach by focusing on providing access to lifelong learning and skills development.

The rising value of knowledge as a commodity cannot be denied as the knowledge intensity of the world economy, along with our ability to distribute knowledge online, is increasing.

Even though significant preparations have been made, South Africa has yet to capitalise on the potential for increased economic competitiveness offered by participation in the global knowledge economy. By acting to create a positive return on investment in knowledge production, dissemination and application, South Africa will be able to enjoy a class of economic growth that is more sustainable over the long term.

Notes and references

1 The author would like to acknowledge the insights of Mike Thoms in compiling this observation.
2 IMD, 'IMD Global Trends Survey 2009'. See www.imd.ch (accessed 29 June 2009).
3 Saramicol Viscardi, 'Artwork that Ideas can Buy'. PSFK, 11 June 2009, www.psfk. com/2009/06/artwork-that-ideas-can-buy.html (accessed 29 June 2009).
4 Don Tapscott and Anthony D. Williams, *Wikinomics* (Penguin Books, 2006).
5 See Hub Culture, www.hubculture.com (accessed 29 June 2009).
6 David Abdulai, 'Managing and Retaining Knowledge Workers in a Hyper-Competitive Era'. UNISA Graduate School of Business Leadership, 2007.
7 Mark Taylor, 'End the University as we Know it'. *The New York Times*, 26 April 2009.

Luci Abrahams, 'South Africa in the Global Knowledge Economy: Structural Irrelevance or Successful New Missions for Development'. LINK Centre, WITS Graduate School of Public and Development Management, 2003.
Stephen Haag, Maeve Cummings and Donald J. McCubbrey, *Management Information Systems for the Information Age* (McGraw Hill, 2006).
John Houghton and Peter Sheehan, 'A Primer on the Knowledge Economy'. Centre for Strategic Economic Studies, Victoria University, 2000.
South Africa's National Research and Development Strategy, Government of the Republic of South Africa, August 2002. See www.dst.gov.za (accessed 29 June 2009).

CONSUMER
MINDSET

FLUX OBSERVATION

Understanding the current consumer mindset

Carina Louw

To ALL retailers, conglomerates, brands, marketers and entrepreneurs: brace yourselves, a consumer revolution is underway. The rapid changes resulting from developments in social media and other new technology mean that consumers have moved beyond merely sampling online communications, services and social networks to making them a way of life.

Meanwhile, the messages of the importance of ethical consumption and sustainability are spreading and radically altering the consumer landscape. In addition, there is a strong backlash against the homogenising effects of globalisation in mature consumer markets, heralding the return of an emphasis on the individual.

These seemingly disparate trends have combined with the global financial crisis and, in a heartbeat, yesterday's conspicuous consumption seems tasteless, even vulgar.

Welcome to the era of the activist consumer, in which a credit card is used as a ballot to vote in or out a product or company based on its social, ethical or environmental standpoint.

Allow me to introduce the consumers of today: the connected consumer, the eco-warrior and the non-conformist.

The connected consumer

Never before have consumers had so much choice and hence power when choosing products. With virtually endless information only a click away, consumers habitually read reviews, share opinions, compare prices, view product details and vent their frustrations about brands in blog posts and on Twitter. Consumers apply 'armchair wisdom' to virtually every offering and are more thorough in their assessment of products and services than most companies themselves have been.

The connected consumer increasingly relies on a network of trusted experts who share their experiences and opinions of brands and services with the online community. This means that one customer's dissatisfaction can spread to potential customers faster than you can say 'bankruptcy'.

Can you really afford to ignore the connected consumer? Think about it: currently there are more than 1.5 billion people worldwide who go online every day, and more than 55 million of these are in Africa.[2] South Africa is set to become as connected as the rest of the developed world with the arrival of the Seacom underwater fibre-optic cable that will bring millions of consumers affordable high-speed Internet access at home and work, in some consumers' cases for the first time.

Mobile broadband is poised to be the next phase of the interactive communications revolution. The number of mobile phone subscriptions worldwide is expected to grow to a staggering 5.6 billion by 2013, half of which will be mobile broadband connections.[3] Africa has more mobile phone subscribers than North America. Can you afford to look at the continent as a global charity case?

Always-on, always-with-you mobile phones place information that was previously difficult to come by at consumers' fingertips. An example of an efficient service solution that provides instant information is Qkey, a new South African communication tool that enables consumers to interact with other consumers and compare

Word of mouth

Sarah Badat

Budgets are tight and billboards are expensive. As traditional channels of marketing and advertising are fast becoming archaic and intrusive it is apparent that brands need to explore more engaging methods to garner customer acceptance. With findings from a study conducted by research company Millward Brown showing that 70% of customers are doubtful that brands tell the truth in advertisements, it is no wonder that consumers are taking a step back and starting to base their purchasing decisions on the opinions of people whom they know and trust.[1]

Word-of-mouth marketing, also known as viral marketing, is fast becoming an essential ingredient in the recipe for a successful marketing campaign. As a result of the economic downturn, brands are starting to explore word-of-mouth marketing as an efficient form of generating customer interest. The Millward Brown study found that 43% of US companies are planning to use word of mouth as a key component of their marketing strategies this year.

Formed in 2004, The Word of Mouth Marketing Association (WOMMA), a USA-based organisation, believes that word-of-mouth marketing is about empowering consumers to share their experiences and harnessing the voice of the customer for the good of the brand. It's also, as WOMMA points out, about acknowledging that unsatisfied customers are equally powerful.

Earlier this year Ford launched The Ford Fiesta Movement. This entailed recruiting 100 Ford Agents from over 4 000 applicants to spend six months behind the wheel of their own Fiestas, sharing their experiences and completing monthly missions to show people what the Ford Fiesta experience is all about. This marketing initiative links products to experiences, putting the power in the hands of consumers who play an integral role in shaping brand image. It also opens the door for consumers to participate in a conversation with the brand.

The traditional practice of word-of-mouth marketing was well entrenched before the boom of mass advertising and it seems as though we have come full circle as viral marketing is taking on an online form to speak to tribes through like-minded forums.

Online word-of-mouth platforms are

TREND SNACK

Word of mouth *continued*

changing the way consumers communicate with each other. Countless social networking and review sites have become places for customers to share advice, opinions and experiences.

Brands are hopping on board to such an extent that many have created full-time positions that require employees to manage social networking services encouraging communication between brand and consumer, over and above doing some damage control if things get messy. As a result of the ease with which information is disseminated online, generating and monitoring online word of mouth is becoming as important, if not more so, than its real-world counterpart. Brand transparency plays a key role in harnessing the power of word of mouth both on- and offline. As consumers are sharing more information about themselves through social media, they are expecting their brands to step up and do the same thing. It's all about talking to your customers in the language they speak and, if you're clever about it, they'll only say good things in return.

T R E N D S N A C K

information on different brands by simply dialling a 'Q-number' found on or in products, such as adverts within magazines, or on product packages.[4]

American iPhone users can point the phone's camera at any product's barcode to access price comparisons from online and brick-and-mortar retailers in the vicinity, allowing the consumer to choose the right product at the right price.

The eco-warrior

The urgent message contained in Al Gore's *An Inconvenient Truth* struck a global nerve, changing the way we think about production and consumption. Questions most people never stopped to ask before are now an integral part of how we live and consume. How was the product made? Who made it? How did it get to its point of sale? What effect will it have on the environment?

Ethics, fair trading, sustainability, climate change and ecology – issues resultant from the 'green effect' – are grouped under the umbrella term 'eco-awareness'.

In early 2008 South Africans experienced crippling power outages and escalating petrol and food prices. As a result, our own version of environmental consciousness became closely associated with using less electricity and less fuel, as well as saving money by purchasing more locally produced, in-season produce (thereby lowering carbon emissions by eliminating the transport necessary for foods to travel to South Africa from around the world).

As conspicuous consumption gives way to ethical consumption, consumers will rely on the provenance and green credentials of a product, which are perhaps becoming the new criteria for a consumers' 'snob factor' influencing purchasing decisions.

The mobile phone revolution has contributed to the eco trend, too. Shoppers at some forward-thinking retailers can now trace the origins of a product using the barcode, thereby monitoring how far a product has had to travel to reach its destination. For example, New Zealand sportswear company Icebreaker allows its customers to check online how merino jerseys from its range were produced – from where the wool originated to who spun the yarn under what working conditions, right back to the individual sheep that supplied the wool. All of this is accessed via what is termed a 'baacode' attached to the garment.[5]

Home-grown vegetables have also become something of a new status symbol, while producing your own preserves or pickles is seen as a quasi-political act. These are all part of the new eco-warrior's way of life. The proliferation of fresh food and vegetable markets around the country is an illustration of how sustainability has become part of the consumer's vernacular.

Whether you are a light-green (part-time) or dark green (full-time, hard-core) eco-warrior, it is certain that becoming more green will be on everyone's radar in the coming years.

The non-conformist

In an era where even distressed jeans are mass-produced, people are yearning for greater customisation and for unique experiences, products and services that cater to their specific preferences and particular tastes.

Consumers are increasingly proud of the idiosyncrasies that are espoused by the products they consume. This trend is not limited to affluent consumers and also spans generations and geographic boundaries. The time for categorising consumers along impersonal demographic lines, such as age, gender and LSMs (Living Standards Measures), is over; it is important to recognise consumers as opinionated individuals with unique values and lifestyles.

Experienced consumers frequently employ a cross-industry mindset when searching for products. Once a particular product raises the quality bar and lowers the price, consumers expect equivalent levels of service and quality across the board.

A recession-induced re-evaluation

The ups and downs of what is termed 'consumer confidence' aside, the global financial crisis has radically altered the affluent consumer's attitude towards spending. Consumption is not magically disappearing; it is merely adjusting to the current zeitgeist as society starts to focus on more mindful consumerism. Big brands are now offering discreet packaging to offset the conspicuousness and potential guilt that is lately associated with shopping. As Martin Lindstrom from Branding Strategy Insider testifies:

> I recently made a small purchase at Hermès, and I was asked if I would prefer to carry it in a plain brown bag without the famous logo. I was somewhat taken aback, and on further inquiry, the assistant replied that I would perhaps feel more comfortable with anonymity. Something as simple as a bag, that only six months ago was the essence of a status symbol now might be considered a liability.[6]

As ostentatious spending is done in shame, and luxury becomes the new porn, many affluent consumers are filing for lifestyle liquidation. Retail trend specialist David Wolfe recently shed light on the situation:

> The numbers are frightening: Retail sales at luxury retailers are down 30%. Luxury brands now confront a consumer who is earning less and saving more in a marketplace where, for the first time in several generations, there is actually some populist revulsion with conspicuous consumption. If we are really living through, as Time magazine proclaimed, 'The End of Excess', then how do companies – indeed, an entire

economy – geared toward excess and aspiration retool and convince weary, debt-burdened consumers disgusted by their own previous spending that their brands are really not about excess at all?[7]

Significantly, the recession has induced large-scale reassessment of values. Consumers are applying higher expectations to the products they buy and now ask: 'Do I really need this?' 'Will it add value to my life?' 'Does it meet my needs?' 'Is it worth the price?'

The message is clear: irresponsible luxury is out and meaningful products and experiences are in.

Thanks to the democratic ethos of social networks, websites like Wikipedia and companies like Threadless, today's consumers are encouraged to *do* as opposed merely to consume. Companies cannot afford to ignore this new brand of active-aggressive consumer, because even after the turbulent times have subsided, consumers will continue to reward or punish brands depending on their social, ethical and environmental standpoints.

The era of engagement

Companies can no longer turn their backs on millions of connected consumers. If you can't beat them, join them, goes the saying, and with a host of interactive technologies available, such as blogs, Twitter and mobile, there are many ways for companies to join the conversation.

The South African website Getclosure is a forum in which consumers may voice displeasure, and in which companies have the opportunity of appeasing customers by responding. It is surprising to see how many companies still simply ignore these complaints. Increasingly, businesses will need to make use of such forums to post their solutions and apologies as promptly as possible. The era of engagement isn't only about handling complaints, it is also about talking to your customer. On the Internet, consumers are able to effortlessly select and customise anything from shower curtains to doggy treats. And they are asking in all honesty why they can't do this in the offline world. This is known as the 'change gap': when a commercial response is too slow to catch up with the changes brought by new technologies. Consumers demand the same level of service and features no matter where or when they decide to shop.

Speak to the tribe

In an increasingly impersonal world people feel the need to connect with like-minded individuals who share the same passions and speak the same language, forming what Seth Godin refers to as 'tribes'. Godin, author of *Tribes, we Need you to Lead us*, argues that the Internet is putting an end to mass marketing because modern communication technology is making it easier for individuals to form meaningful groups.[8]

It is important to identify these niche groups and to create products and services customised to their needs. Speak the consumer language of the tribe by telling consumers what they want to hear and incorporating product features tailored for their distinct lifestyles. Consumers will see the brand as relevant and reward you.

Go the extra mile

Compared with lowering prices, adding extra features to services and products is a far more effective way to lure consumers. It also creates a perception about the value of a brand. This can be anything from a regular freebie (but make it something that they actually want), to reward systems, to extra privileges that add innovative forms of convenience or status to their lives. For example, South African health insurance company Discovery offers a wellness program called Vitality that rewards clients for choosing a healthier lifestyle. Members receive points for decreasing their health risks, such as quitting smoking or cutting down on drinking. The more points a member has, the higher the status (bronze, silver, gold or diamond), the more benefits, such as discounts at grocery stores, they receive.

Some brands are taking the concept of added perks a step further by paying customers to promote their brand, giving money in return for old products or allowing customers to sell their products.

Be real, be true

As consumers make purchasing decisions based on values in addition to wants and needs, they will demand greater authenticity and complete transparency from brands. At this stage the consumer's mindset is jittery and distrustful. So if you say that your product is authentic, it had better be, since informed, connected consumers can see right through sales tactics like 'greenwashing' (disingenuously making your products appear more eco-friendly than they really are); adding a 'Made in Italy' label (when it was actually mass produced on an assembly line) or calling something a 'best offer' (when in fact it's the same offer but with hidden costs). Consumers will reward companies that are transparent and penalise those who aren't.

Constant distraction, information overload, a larger workload, time-starvation, borderline burnout, endless variety, guilt, choice paralysis, recession, job scarcity, high inflation, debt: these are all daily familiarities of the average consumer. After years of training in hyper-consumption, the new generation of activist consumers is ready to fight to get precisely what they want. If you help them to do this, you are well on your way.

Notes and references

1 Matabello Motloun, 'Marketing: A Personal Opinion'. *Financial Mail*, 29 May 2009.
2 Cellular News, 'Global Mobile Phone Users Top 3.3 Billion by end of 2007'. See www.cellular-news.com/story/31352.php (accessed 21 July 2009).
3 Cellular News, 'Worldwide Mobile Subscriptions to Reach 5.6 Billion by 2013'.
4 See Qkey, www.qkey.co.za (accessed 20 July 2009).
5 See www.icebreaker.com/site/baacode/index.html (accessed 21 July 2009).
6 Martin Lindstrom, 'The End of Brands as we Know them?' Branding Strategy Insider, 18 February 2009, www.brandingstrategyinsider.com/2009/02/the-end-of-brands-as-we-know-them.html (accessed 29 May 2009).
7 Karl Taro Greenfeld, 'Luxe Redux'. Reuters, 8 July 2009, www.reuters.com/article/bigMoney/idUS328761657920090708 (accessed 21 July 2009).
8 Seth Godin, *Tribes, we Need you to Lead us* (Piatkus Books, 2008).

Kurt Andersen, 'The End of Excess: Is this Crisis Good for America?' Time Online, 26 March 2009, www.time.com/time/nation/article/0,8599,1887728,00.html (accessed 20 April 2009).
Kate Betts, 'Fire Sale: Once Towering, the Luxury Market Teeters'. Time Online, 7 June 2009, www.time.com/time/business/article/0,8599,1903253,00.html (accessed 21 July 2009).
'Industry Facts and Figures'. See www.clickatell.com/press/facts_figures.php#1 (accessed 21 July 2009).

Internet World Stats, 'Usage and Population Statistics'. See www.internetworldstats.com/stats.htm (accessed 29 May 2009).

Ruth La Ferla, 'Even in Recession, Spend they Must: Luxury Shoppers Anonymous'. The New York Times Online, 10 December 2008, www.nytimes.com/2008/12/11/fashion/11PRIVATE.html?_r=3 (accessed 28 May 2009).

Sameer Reddy, 'Luxury Brands Cope with an Image Problem.' *Newsweek*, 17 April 2009, www.newsweek.com/id/194553 (accessed 26 May 2009).

Johnnie L. Roberts, 'Luxury Shame, Why even the Very Rich are Cutting back on Conspicuous Consumption'. Newsweek Online, 8 December 2008, www.newsweek.com/id/171246 (accessed 26 May 2009).

'The Wealthy Turn Stealthy as Economy Weakens'. MSNBC online, 27 January 2009, www.msnbc.msn.com/id/28878147/ (accessed 28 May 2009).

FLUX OBSERVATION

The empathetic economy

Loren Phillips

Eᴍᴘᴀᴛʜʏ, ᴇᴛʜɪᴄꜱ and intuition are characteristics that we do not readily associate with the cut-throat corporate world, but critics of current business practices agree that these are exactly the characteristics we need to infuse into the structures of power, to build a more inclusive economy, and to benefit consumers as well as those who cannot afford to participate in the global economy.

British-born economic thinker and activist James Robertson has been developing theories in economic and social reform since the 1970s. During a visit to South Africa in 1996, Robertson set up the South Africa New Economics Network (SANE). Robertson, the author of a number of books on this topic, defines two possible responses to shifts taking place in the world: the Hyper-Expansive (HE) Economy, and the Sane Humane, Ecological (SHE) Economy. According to Robertson:

> The conventional idea of progress, with indiscriminate economic growth, socially and environmentally damaging globalisation, and remote government decisions closely linked to the interests of business and finance, is not a possible way forward. It's not enough now to say the future doesn't have to be like that. It can't be like that. Those who think it can are leading the world to disaster on a catastrophic scale.[1]

Issues such as sustainable development, social and economic justice and 'environmentally benign' progress are the ingredients for a successful future. Looking at Robertson's concept of the SHE economy, which is based on caring and social consciousness, backed up by community values and intuition, it becomes apparent that these traits have so far been undervalued in business practice, and it is now time to call on them to build a brave new world.

The new age

There have been several indicators of a significant paradigm shift in the way companies are run, possibly expedited by recent events in the global economy. The first and most marked indicator of a worldwide shift in thinking was the election of the president of the USA, Barack Obama, who, in his inaugural address, attributed the weakened American economy to greed and irresponsibility. He also spoke of a 'new age' based on social concern and respect for one another and our world.[2] Since his inauguration, Obama has clearly expressed his strong family values and makes a point of listening to the people he serves. His fresh and compassionate approach stands in stark contrast to the Bush administration, which showed a flagrant disregard for public sentiment.

From governmental structures to the profitable private sector, we are seeing a greater concern for people and the world at large. A temporary pause in the grind of industry, such as the slowdown in vehicle manufacturing that has brought Detroit to its knees, has allowed issues concerning the future of the planet and the scarcity of resources to surface. Current consumption patterns have been thrown into question and alternatives are being sought in an attempt to slow an almost-certain ecological catastrophe.

In June 2008, the Microsoft co-founder Bill Gates bowed out of his position at the helm of the multi-billion dollar global corporation

in order to focus more time and energy on the day-to-day operations of the philanthropic Bill and Melinda Gates Foundation. In an
article in *Time*, Gates talked passionately about an alternative business model that is more inclusive of the poor and the marginalised.
He called it 'Creative Capitalism', and proposed how companies
could strive to be innovative and devise solutions to some of the
world's most devastating problems, such as hunger, poverty and
HIV/AIDS.[3]

Social concern of this kind has a strikingly feminine tone, if we
consider the traditional role of women as caregivers and nurtur-
ers. In order to move forward and build a sustainable way of life for
all, government and big business need to do more to invest in and
support the communities of which they are part. At every level of
society people need to start caring more. And this seems to be happening already.

A tipping point has been reached in the way middle-income-
to-affluent consumers make their purchase decisions. Increasingly,
these decisions are based on a brand's social stance. More consumers are actively seeking to support companies that do more than
just business. One example is Tom's, a California-based shoe company that promises to donate one pair of shoes to a child in need for
every pair bought. This company is attracting a new group of shoppers who care about contributing positively to poor communities.

If companies are to benefit from new consumer sentiment, there
are a few things they need to pay attention to, so as not to be left
behind in an increasingly hyper-aware and expectant economy.
Consumers seek more participation with brands, to be part of the
conversation rather than the recipient of a brand's message. The
systems and manufacturing left-brain logic is giving way to a more
inclusive approach, guided by wisdom, intuition and knowledge.

Getting women on [the] board

For decades, women have been trying to compete in business according to male-defined rules. In a recent article published in *The New York Times*, opinion writer Nicholas D. Kristof focused on Wall Street as a traditionally male-dominated bastion of business.[4]

Kristof cited a study conducted in Britain among traders that measured testosterone levels in men, in relation to profits. It found that these levels were associated with increased risk-taking behaviour; which tends to result in greater rewards. Conversely, this also can mean bigger losses. In light of these findings, Kristof posed the question: 'Was the primary problem in the recent fallout on Wall Street a case of elevated testosterone, instead of the subprime mortgage disaster?'[5]

In fact, a popular question bandied about by opinion writers and analysts subsequent to these events was: 'Would the economic crisis have happened if women had been in charge – if Lehman Brothers had been Lehman Sisters instead?'[6]

Kristof also cites a paper published in the *Journal of Economic Theory* that states: 'There seems to be a strong consensus that diverse groups perform better at problem solving', as opposed to homogenous groups.[7]

Now, it's a little simplistic to let the blame rest solely on the shoulders of our testosterone-fuelled brothers. The problem is not that they were all men, but that they formed a homogeneous group and homogenous groups can be easily led astray: members tend to think and react in similar ways, and do not have the benefit of different perspectives to contrast with their own.

It seems that a more varied approach is needed in steering a large ship of industry. Boards including women seem to be faring better through the crisis than those led by men only. The '2007 Catalyst Census of Women Board Directors of the Fortune 500' survey[8] showed that there is a direct and positive relationship between the average number of female board members and chief officers and the companies standing in the top 500 (in terms of gross revenue). More and more, boards are taking on women to share valuable insights into one of the most powerful consumer markets today: women.

'Womenomics'

The 21st-century woman has realised that she can have it all: a fulfilling career and a loving family. It is no longer a question of one or the other, and in order to retain the talent and skills that a woman can offer to an organisation, companies are loosening up to allow more flexibility within the workplace.

'Womenomics'[10] is the theory that women play a primary role in economic growth. It refers to a 'paradigm shift in the way individuals and companies approach work, due to an increase in value of women in the workforce and changing attitudes of women towards priorities of balancing work and personal life'.[11] The term was coined in 1995, in reference to a study commissioned by car manufacturer Chrysler to assess the buying power of women. According to the study, women accounted for 80% of purchase decisions in the USA.

And it is not only women who are attempting to redefine the rules of work and negotiate a better balance, but more men and young people too. This is especially apparent in the hyper-mobile IT industry. Start-ups like Google and Facebook have single-handedly changed the face of work for an entire generation of young workers. Facebook, for example, promotes a flat corporate structure within its open-plan

Marketing to women

Loren Phillips

A few years ago South African entrepreneurs began dabbling in marketing products specifically designed to appeal to women. This was in keeping with a worldwide trend. Among the early starters was 1st for Women, a company offering insurance products tailored to a female clientele. The company maintains that women are safer and more responsible drivers than men, and thus a better insurance risk. Based on this premise, 1st for Women was able to offer lower premiums to women drivers.

In its report 'Female Fever', leading trends website Trendwatching.com highlighted a focus on female shoppers through targeted product offerings such as tools and travel packages designed for women in particular. The report states that prior to this, women had been an underserved 'mega-niche', yet made up a group who controls most of the purchase decisions in the USA. With this in mind, it is easy to see how catering to this market would be in a company's best interests.

Websites have been established to service this growing need to capture the female market. TrendSight, for example, offers opinions and insights on marketing to women. Locally, Women24 speaks to South African women about a range of topics that have bearing on the life of women – everything from beauty to pregnancy. Servicing women and their needs is also gaining traction in the blogosphere, which hosts BlogHer, a portal devoted to female bloggers and Marketing to Women Online, a blog about what women really want.

Women are responsible for 80% of the purchase decisions in the average household.[9] On average, women enter more willingly into conversations around brands and products and give feedback more freely than men. They prefer collaboration, networking and peer-to-peer interaction because women, in general, are more focused on building and maintaining relationships whereas men tend to be more focused on the end transaction. Owing to the depth of the relationships that women form, they demand a high level of honesty, trust and transparency from the brands that they choose. It is no longer a case of build-it-and-they-will-buy; it is a matter of garnering feedback from customers and using this

TREND SNACK

Marketing to women *continued*

to create an improved, more functional product.

Women are often social creatures and any way of connecting with them and enabling them to connect with other women will be rewarded with positive brand sentiment and ensuing engagement. Stimulating the conversation is also an invaluable tool for gauging women's attitudes to and opinions on a product or its functionality.

Marketers need to remember that word of mouth is still one of the most powerful drivers of purchases and women being social, conversational beings, like to talk. Women operate by referral, and enjoy sharing opinions about products and services.

The social web has opened up a multitude of platforms on which people can share their opinions and ideas on any subject, no matter how seemingly obscure. From the brand side, various tools like Google Alerts now allow brands to 'listen' in on what people are saying about them, alerting them every time their name is used in an online article or blog post. This is an invaluable method of tracking up-to-the-minute feedback on a company's brand, and it opens up the opportunity for a company to respond to negative 'talk' swiftly and decisively.

Women are using social network services and blogs to engage with other women in a more conversational way. These social networks are an online expression of the way women operate in real life. They are hard-wired to form communities, which is exactly what makes social media sites tick. It is clear (from how advertising has not been the answer to monetising sites like Facebook and Twitter) that brands cannot simply barge in on the conversation, but need to find a way of making their voices heard, with honesty and in a more human way that engenders trust rather than churning out the 'market speak' that has worked up until now.

T R E N D S N A C K

warehouse-like office, where all are treated like equals working to-wards a common cause. Employees are attended by world-class chefs and are encouraged to skateboard to meetings. There are also beds and kitchens that employees can make use of freely. Employees can come and go as they please, with transport costs covered by the company. This 'feel-good' atmosphere boosts productivity and employee loyalty, making Facebook a really nice place to work.

It has been shown that flexi-time can also increase productivity, making this a sensible solution for businesses. Locally, IBM South Africa has a very progressive policy on fostering female talent in the workplace. Senior female managers make up over 25% of the executive team, and the company is focused on empowering women through mentorship programmes. According to the website 'Top Women in Business and Government',[12] IBM promotes a work ethic that encompasses flexibility, mobility and outcome-based performance measurement.

Women often leave their jobs to focus on raising a family, and companies lose out on their talent. According to Katty Kay and Claire Shipman in their recently published book, *Womenomics: Write your own Rules for Success*, women tend to spend more time pursuing tertiary education and leave with more qualifications than their male counterparts, making them valuable assets to a company.[13]

A new model for work is slowly being etched into corporate thinking, which allows for more time to devote to family and life, increasing overall happiness and creating a sense of accomplishment, which ultimately leads to better performance in the workplace.

So, as feminine values are beginning to redefine business thinking, women themselves are beginning to play a larger, more important role in the business world. Women account for more top jobs than ever before and female entrepreneurs, such as Natalie Massenet of retail site Net-a-Porter.com fame, are carving out brand new positions in the market.

The triumph of good

The business rules are being rewritten, this time with women on a more equal footing. The Hyper-Expansive economic model has proved itself exhausted and incapable of addressing the pressing issues of a growing wealth gap between rich and poor. It has also led to an alarming depletion of the Earth's essential resources for the benefit of a few. If we can superimpose a more Sane, Humane and Ecological model, which shows concern for the Earth and its precious resources as well as caring for each other at the same time, a more sustainable future can be designed.

We are already seeing the early signs of change. The figurative carpet of power has been yanked from under the feet of major institutions and global corporate entities, and is being put back in the hands of many, aided exponentially by the connections and networks that the web affords.

Feminine attributes such as community-building, caring, nurturing and making decisions based on wisdom and intuition are a fitting response in the workplace to the greedy and selfish ways that have dominated until now and have been shown to be unsuccessful.

The values and ethics evident in this empathetic economy signpost the way towards building a more inclusive future. This model exalts honesty and integrity over half-truths and greed, and creation and nurturing over destruction. It is more transparent in practice, and seeks to do well for the benefit of all.

Notes and references

1   James Robertson, 'Working for a SANE Alternative'. See www.jamesrobertson.com (accessed 20 January 2009).

2   Barack Obama, 'Barack Obama's Inaugural Address'. The New York Times Online,
    20 January 2009, www.nytimes.com/2009/01/20/us/politics/20textobama.
    html?pagewanted=1&_r=2 (accessed 20 January 2009).

3   Bill Gates, 'Making Capitalism More Creative'. *Time*, 31 July 2008.

4   Nicholas D. Kristof, 'Mistresses of the Universe'. The New York Times Online,
    7 February 2009, www.nytimes.com/2009/02/08/opinion/08kristof.
    html?scp=1&sq=mistresses%20of%20the%20universe&st=cse%3E (accessed
    3 February 2009).

5   Kristof, 'Mistresses of the Universe'.

6   Judith Orr, 'Lehman Sisters?' *Socialist Review*, March 2009, www.socialistreview.
    org.uk/article.php?articlenumber=10747 (accessed 22 July 2009); also, Judy
    Rosener, 'Women on Corporate Boards Makes Good Business Sense'. Women's
    Media, 2 April 2009, www.womensmedia.com/lead/87-women-on-corporate-
    boards-makes-good-business-sense.html (accessed 22 July 2009).

7   Kristof, 'Mistresses of the Universe'.

8   Catalyst Inc., '2007 Catalyst Census of Women Board Directors of the Fortune
    500', December 2007, www.catalyst.org/publication/12/2007-catalyst-census-
    of-women-board-directors-of-the-fortune-500 (accessed 24 July 2009).

9   Jonathan Bell, 'FemTech Design'. *Viewpoint*, December 2008, Issue 23: The
    Eve-olution Issue, p. 101.

10 Paul McFedries, 'Womenomics'. Wordspy, 11 December 2007, www.wordspy.
    com/words/womenomics.asp (accessed 19 June 2009).

11 See www.en.wikipedia.org/wiki/Womenomics (accessed 19 June 2009).

12 Top Women in Business and Government, 'Top Women in Business and
    Government'. See www.businesswomen.co.za/Companies/ibm.asp (accessed
    19 June 2009).

13 Katty Kay and Claire Shipman, *Womenomics: Write your own Rules for Success*
    (HarperCollins, 2009).

Ruth Sunderland, 'The Real Victims of this Credit Crunch? Women'. The Guardian
    Online, 18 January 2009, www.guardian.co.uk/lifeandstyle/2009/jan/18/
    women-credit-crunch-ruth-sunderland (accessed 22 July 2009).

FLUX OBSERVATION

Redeeming the reputation of luxury

Dion Chang

THE LUXURY brand industry is in trouble. The role-players all know it despite the brave faces. Some acknowledge it while others blame the global financial crisis for the downturn in sales. The truth is that while the financial crisis has contributed significantly to lacklustre sales, the foundations on which this industry stands started to sway long before this.

Guy Salter, the Deputy Chairman of Walpole (a British luxury goods association) was recently quoted as saying: 'There is a luxury fatigue going on which predates economic concerns.'[1] The logocrazed era is coming to an end and the global recession will serve as a stark reminder that the party is indeed over. A new world awaits and with it comes a new value system.

It's no secret that since 2004 luxury brands have shifted their focus from their traditional First World markets to emerging markets in developing countries. Countries such as China, Russia, India and even South Africa have seen a rash of luxury brand stores appearing in upmarket shopping centres or in malls especially created for them. These new markets have ensured that there has been some growth, albeit slight, for the more aggressive players.

Luxury brand consultants Bain & Company predicted a 4% drop in growth (from a 6.5% level) for 2008, while Altagamma (the trade association of the Italian luxury industry) predicted a sales decline in the USA of 15%. In an interview with *Fortune* the CEO of Yves Saint Laurent, Valerie Hermann, went so far as to call the current economic climate, not so much a financial crisis, but a 'crisis of values'.[2]

The article continued: 'Even after the global economy stabilizes, will anyone want US$2 000 handbags or US$5 000 watches? Or is there a risk that "luxury" will go the way of yuppies and become a fad many would prefer to forget?'[3]

Some people in the luxury brands business scoff at such a notion, arguing that there will always be a market for luxury goods. I couldn't agree more, but there is some truth in labelling luxury (as we currently know it) as simply a 'fad'.

The downside of democracy

Almost all of today's luxury brands started out as small, family-run businesses that built their reputation and credibility one hand-sewn stitch at a time. Exclusivity, craftsmanship and quality have always been the cornerstones of the luxury industry. It is the same allure that drives men to commission a bespoke suit from Saville Row, or women to order a designer couture gown.

Luxury is elitist, and unashamedly so: and that's the whole point. The *New Penguin English Dictionary* defines luxury as 'something desirable but costly or difficult to obtain',[4] and today luxury branded items are no longer difficult to obtain, only relatively costly, and so desirable that well-made fakes have become ubiquitous. Often they are hard to differentiate from the real thing, and are as socially acceptable. What went wrong?

The answer lies in the rejuvenation of many of today's top luxury brands during the late 1980s and early 90s. Ironically, many of the traditional luxury brands were reinvented because they had become devalued due to the numerous accessory licences the brands had sold off. It is what essentially killed a brand like Pierre Cardin.

One of the first things that Gucci had to do before reinventing itself was to rein in or buy out all the licensees it had originally sold the brand off to.

High-profile designers such as Tom Ford, John Galliano, Alexander McQueen and Marc Jacobs were tasked with reinventing traditional but tired brands such as Gucci, Dior, Givenchy and Louis Vuitton, which they did with great success. Spurred on by this creative and, more importantly, financial rejuvenation, many brands focused their energies on a lower rung of the consumer ladder – the upper (but still mass) middle market. To do this, luxury brands once again focused on accessories, especially handbags, to provide a broader appeal.

Much like perfume or designer underwear, handbags afford entry into the luxury brand world at a fraction of the cost of the brand's other product offerings. Karl Lagerfeld acknowledged this, saying: 'Everyone can afford a luxury handbag', and Miuccia Prada agreed. She explained in an interview:

> With the bag, there are no leftovers because there are no sizes, unlike shoes or clothes. It is easier to choose a bag than a dress because you don't have to face the age, the weight … all those problems. And there is an obsession with bags. It's so easy to make money. The bag is the miracle of the company.[5]

Handbags pulled in the money – and the necessary hype – for all luxury brands. In Japan (the world's largest consumer of luxury brands), 'over 90% of … women in their twenties own a Louis Vuitton item!'[6] It was the aim of the luxury industry to 'democratise' luxury, and to make luxury 'more accessible' … and it succeeded. For Bernard Arnault, Chairman and CEO of the LVMH group, one of the ways to achieve this 'democratisation' was 'to make consumers buy luxury branded items not for what they are, but for what they represent'.[7]

And therein lies the downfall of the luxury branded item. Between 2000 and 2005 there was an extensive roll out of luxury branded stores worldwide. To feed these outlets and the mass middle market they catered for, an accelerated fashion cycle came into play. Every six months a new must-have 'it' bag or accessory was launched to keep the devotees hungry for more. The downside of this strategy was the accumulation of seasonal 'dead stock'.

In the traditional world of luxury brands, design cycles were slower and design styles more iconic, resulting in a longer shelf-life for many of the products. With luxury brands feeding off the fashion treadmill, the phrase 'so last season' has become an expensive reality. Luxury brands have fuelled the fickle passions of the label victim and are being lumped with more and more out-of-fashion stock at the end of each season. This stock is routed to various 'outlet' stores around the world, such as Desert Hills Premium Outlets, just two hours outside Los Angeles, where it is then sold off at discounted prices – sometimes up to 75% off the original. So much for exclusivity.

Austerity is the new black

The strategy to 'democratise luxury' worked and share prices of luxury companies shot through the roof, even though the industry was slowly cannibalising its own worth. This strategy did not, however, factor in a global economic crisis where the people who were most affected were the same consumers the luxury brands had targeted so aggressively. When strapped for cash, the mass middle markets were forced to reassess their purchases, and weigh up luxury items versus necessities. The knock-on effect on luxury branded items has been devastating.

But even for the super rich – whom many believed to be impervious to the global recession – luxury brands have lost their allure by going mass market. In the 2009 Luxury Institute survey[8] a surprising change of mood had taken hold.

In its sample of 500-plus high net-worth consumers, the Institute discovered that:

❏ 64% of wealthy consumers believe luxury goods prices are too high relative to the value they deliver;
❏ Superior quality (82%), superior craftsmanship (78%) and superior customer service (60%) are the top three requirements of a luxury brand; and
❏ More than 33% of consumers say luxury brands are weaker today than in the recent past at delivering superior customer service and do not have salespeople who are knowledgeable experts about their products.

However, the most surprising finding was how the state of the global economy had altered these consumers' perceptions of conspicuous consumption:

> *Up to 62% of wealthy consumers said that the current state of the economy had changed their view of the luxury industry. Key reasons included: being more budget-conscious, luxury goods too 'mass' vs. price, a sense that flaunting luxury at this time is insensitive, and a desire to help others rather than spend money on themselves.*[9]

The global recession is indeed having a remarkable impact on people's attitudes. Heavily branded luxury items for the sake of status and expression of wealth are increasingly looking out of step with the mood of the world.

The future lies in the past

The signs of change are already evident. Design cycles have started to slow. Designers have started dabbling with 'season-less' collections. Yves Saint Laurent was the first luxury brand to launch a collection (Edition 24) that was specifically designed to last for more than one season, and at a lower price point.

At retail level consumer demand is echoing the need for considered consumption, especially in the upper middle market, which can no longer afford inflated luxury brand prices. In tough times, products that are unique and require discretionary spending – a category in which all luxury branded items fall – suffer the most, and consumers downscale to the next level. Market consultants call this trend 'a flight to quality', where there is a lower frequency in purchases, but of a higher value.

Flux calls this the 'boutique benchmark' and it will become evident across all industries. Consumers will stop spending at the lowest and highest ends of the spectrum and look for a combination of quality and value. However, should the product offer a more timeless or classic design, as well as a high quality or durable fabric, then the consumer will be prepared to spend a little more on that purchase.

Ironically, this is the very same principle on which all luxury brands built their reputations: iconic design, superb craftsmanship, reputation and, most importantly, exclusivity.

Armando Branchini, the head of Altagamma, explains the allure of luxury in this way:

> With luxury, it's the product plus the brand ... The values come from the brand, but the product must embody the brand's values in its conception and creation. You lose the myth when the content is no longer consistent with the values. Pierre Cardin was killed because the product no longer contained the values in the brand, and also because the values expressed are no longer interesting for today's customer. Then it becomes just a product.[10]

Luxury in the 21st century has been basically reduced to a product; just a logo-splattered commodity that loses its value with the ebb and flow of fashion's whim. In order for the industry to redeem itself it needs to return not only to the core principles of what luxury items represent, but also needs to capture the new mood of the world and its new definitions of luxury.

Luxury brands have in essence let marketing and advertising run ahead of the product. Freelance luxury bag designer Carol Lipton agrees: 'Luxury is not about innovating designs, it's about innovating advertising. It's more about the brand and not the design, and without the design you get away from all the know-how, the *savoir faire*, and from the craftsmanship.'[11]

And it seems the luxury brands are starting to go back to basics. In a recent interview Gucci CEO Patrizio di Marco said: '[Consumers] want products with substance and good prices. We don't need 75 variations on the same handbag. Two or three are enough.'[12]

One luxury brand that has steadfastly adhered to traditional luxury principles is Hermès, with its iconic Kelly and Birkin bags. The bags' designs have remained unchanged for nearly a century and

Haute grazing

Rutger-Jan van Spaandonk

On a recent trip to Paris and London, some of my favourite food capitals of the world, I was pleased to find that 'grazing' has finally reached the pinnacle of fine dining. And with a bit of luck (and advocacy on my part) this trend will soon hit our shores.

It is too early to foretell the death of the standard three-course meal, but the tales of travellers who have experienced the liberating and unconstrained style of eating at, for example, L'Atelier de Joël Robuchon in Paris or Gordon Ramsay's Maze in London, will hopefully force South Africa's top restaurateurs to rethink the way in which they gastronomically entertain their clientele.

Grazing or the eating of many different small dishes is not new and many credit Spanish tapas-style snacking with its advent, although I believe Asian cuisine to be the true progenitor of this type of dining. Whether experiencing it as Chinese, Indian, Japanese or Thai cookery, the idea is to share a multitude of courses with other table guests, in order to savour multifarious tastes and ingredients.

It is therefore no surprise that grazing first became popular through modern Asian, fusion-style restaurants, such as Takami in Los Angeles and Haiku in Cape Town. The one problem with grazing, though, is that you have to share your food, which is not always ideal for a first date or a business dinner.

Some avant-garde restaurants, such as The Tasting Room in Franschhoek, have tried to incorporate the grazing concept into their repertoire by way of six- to eight-course tasting menus. And very upscale Japanese restaurants, such as Michelin Star-studded Yamazato in Amsterdam, have always had their full-blown *Kaiseki* menus (still communal, but more formal than regular meals).

Although these so-called *menus de dégustation* offer a wide variety of dishes, you cannot really individualise your meal since they are set menus. And that is where I think 'haute grazing' – as I term it – is truly innovative: chefs leave it to their diners to put their own tasting menu together from a long list of delectable small creations. They provide the palette (the choice of dishes and wine) and canvas (the facility

T R E N D S N A C K

Haute grazing *continued*

and ambience), if you will, and it is up to your creativity, imagination and courage how far you take your culinary expedition. Call it Cuisine 2.0: the user-generated dining experience.

You are now the choreographer of the menu and hence the co-producer of the feast. The food takes centre stage. It is no longer just nourishment, or a mere distraction for the human interaction around the table. It takes curiosity and a certain level of culinary knowledge to marry dishes confidently at the opposite sides of the taste spectrum, and still find matching wines. And you have to be enough of a gourmand to want to talk extensively about the whirlwind of flavours and textures. But it is all so very worth it.

So, to all gourmet establishments I say: 'Bring it on!'

T R E N D S N A C K

are still made to order, requiring a waiting period of a few months. The luxury retailer has even resorted to breeding its own crocodiles to keep up with the demand for its iconic handbags. Depending on what combination of skin, hardware, colour and seam construction the buyer specifies, each bag is unique but instantly recognisable ... without a trace of a logo. They are desired not because they are in fashion, but because they will never go out of fashion.

To appeal to a mass market, luxury brands hitched a ride on the fashion carousel and in doing so blurred too many boundaries. Karl Lagerfeld, the Kaiser of modern fashion understands where those boundaries need to lie. In 2004 he collaborated with Swedish mass-market fashion chain H&M to produce an inexpensive range that sold out immediately: a parallel universe from his work at Chanel. He was out to prove a point: that inexpensive can be fabulous too. 'In the end good fashion isn't about price,' he said, 'it's all about taste.'

Notes and references

1 Claire Bell, 'Guccisma'. A report commissioned by Scottish fund management firm Baillie Gifford, 2008.

2 Peter Gumble, 'Luxe in Flux'. *Fortune*, 1 September 2008.

3 Gumble, 'Luxe in Flux'.

4 *New Penguin English Dictionary*, 2nd edition (Penguin Books, 2003).

5 Dana Thomas, *Deluxe: How Luxury Lost its Luster* (Penguin Books, 2007).

6 David Shah, 'The Middle Fights Back'. *Textile View*, 2008.

7 Thomas, *Deluxe*.

8 Luxury Institute LLC, 'Luxury Institute's Wealth and Luxury Trends'. See www.luxuryinstitute.com/trends09.html (accessed 1 June 2009).

9 Luxury Institute LLC, 'Luxury Institute's Wealth and Luxury Trends'.

10 Bell, 'Guccisma'.

11 Bell, 'Guccisma'.

12 Sarah Gay Foden, 'Gucci Renews GG-Logo Purses Priced below $3,000 under New Chief'. Bloomberg.com, 1 June 2009, www.bloomberg.com/apps/news?pid=20601205&sid=a0JlxwMQZD.I 9 (accessed 1 July 2009).

Lauren Milligan, 'Miss Perfect'. Vogue.com, 2 June 2009, www.vogue.co.uk/news/daily/090602-patrizio-di-marco-praises-frida-gia.aspx (accessed 25 June 2009).

Newsweek Special Issue: The Case for Luxury, 6–13 April 2009.

Jonathan Tepperman, 'A Few Good Shirts'. *Newsweek*, 28 March 2009.

LIFESTYLE

REVIEW

The social web and South Africa's emerging digital citizen

Are social media changing the world?

Mike Stopforth

Mike Stopforth is an entrepreneur, writer and public speaker who helps companies extract value from Web 2.0 trends and technologies to create smarter, more profitable businesses. He heads up Cerebra, South Africa's leading social media company, which enjoys relationships with numerous local and global brands, including Toyota, Standard Bank, Rand Merchant Bank, Samsung Mobile, ABSA, Converse, ASCO (Calvin Klein), Zurich, Hollard and Telesure. These and other companies have used Cerebra to connect more meaningfully with their consumers outside the corporate firewall in an era that has reinvented the rules of marketing.

Stopforth is a technology commentator for popular business and marketing websites. He lectures at the Vega School of Branding and features as a guest lecturer on executive programmes at the Graduate School of Business, the Gordon Institute of Business Science and the UNISA School for Business Leadership. He is a popular fixture on the local and international business-to-business speaking circuit and has appeared on numerous radio and TV programmes.

He co-founded web start-up Afrigator, Africa's social media aggregator, and the 27-dinner social networking movement. He blogs at www.mikestopforth.com and can be found on Twitter.

'SOUTH AFRICA does not know what broadband is.' Well at least, not until now. These words belonging to Brian Herlihy, the CEO of Seacom (the visionary company bringing a new undersea cable to South Africa's east coast), are not surprising to anyone who has had the privilege of sampling the mind-blowing connectivity that First World countries call normal. The figures are staggering.

Telkom's high-end offering currently promises 4 megabits per second (MB/s) data speeds to the home, and yet if the end-user gets 100 kilobits per second (KB/s) it's a lot. By comparison, Japanese broadband users enjoy speeds of up to 160MB/s.

Earlier this year, Herlihy took a group of excited journalists and Internet geeks to the Seacom cable station, a few hundred metres from the Mtunzini beachfront in KwaZulu-Natal.

The sad truth is that South Africans have no concept of what the Internet experience is like because of our current level of infrastructure. That will change when Seacom's cable connects to it. Just a few tiny fibres in a protective casing with a circumference no greater than your wrist, this US$600 million digital lifeline is likely to force local providers to lower prices drastically, upscale infrastructure (now you know who to blame for all the roadworks) and do away with data caps. Always-on, unlimited, truly broadband Internet connectivity is literally weeks away as I write and you need to be ready for the tidal wave of change that it will bring.

More mobile than ever

From a trend perspective there may be no other space that requires as much attention and adaptation as that of technology – owing largely to the sheer rate of change that you and I are subjected to on a daily basis.

Laptops are getting thinner and more powerful. A big trend in the last year has been the widespread adoption of so-called net-books (lightweight, scaled-down laptops) as the weapon of choice for the connected, nomadic urban professional. It beats lugging that 4-kilogram grey monster around with you. Instead, a sexy little white Asus or Lenovo netbook is the same size as your Moleskine, and weighs less than 1 kilogram.

Mobile phones are portable music players, 8 megapixel cameras, Global Positioning System (GPS) devices and web browsers rolled into one – a far cry from the monochromatic weapons of self-defence you and I wielded just over ten years ago. A war is being waged at the bleeding edge of smartphone technology between kingpins Apple (with its iPhone still regarded by many as the market leader), Nokia, BlackBerry, Samsung and HTC.

Sadly, in the race to be first with the flashiest camera, or coolest email technology, many of these phones go to market with wobbly operating systems, meaning that the user experience is really only realised after the third or fourth firmware update. Once again, Apple leads the pack in this regard with its solid-as-a-rock operating system, followed closely by the ever-popular Symbian S60, owned and managed by Nokia and licensed by other cellphone makers. Google's Linux-based Android OS, now being experienced for the first time on devices locally is showing great potential, while Windows Mobile, quite frankly, continues to disappoint.

Meet the prosumer

It's not just our gadgets that are evolving rapidly. The World Wide Web, on the back of a whole new generation of users, is morphing into a beast far removed from the platform that fostered the dot-com crash of the late 1990s.

From a business perspective the most intriguing and challenging trend has been the emergence of so-called social media – a set of tools and technologies on the web that has, in the past three or four years, done a lot more than make words like 'blog', 'Facebook' and 'Susan Boyle' household terms.

Social media have fundamentally changed the way we all do business. It's ironic. We took years to adapt to the web and all the possibilities it offered us in terms of business, and just when we got the hang of it, things changed again.

Let me state this categorically: you know everything you need to know about Web 2.0, social media, social networking, consumer-generated media (pick your buzzword), blogs, wikis and even that Twitter thing.

I say that because too many companies that I address, too many teams that I consult to, and too many individuals that I connect with assume that they need to be able to write pages of code, or have some other-worldly grasp on the technological component of these new platforms to be able to understand them and benefit from them.

Code is a commodity. Community, however, is priceless. Wondering why Facebook recently sneezed at a US$10 billion valuation of its ever-expanding social networking platform? It's got nothing to do with some secret that lies hidden in the ones and zeros that make up the software that run the site. There are no eleven herbs and spices here. In fact, you can download a script online for US$100

Micro-blogging

Mike Stopforth

Micro-blogging, or micro-publishing, is an emerging trend that has taken not only the tech world but the world of politics and big media by storm. Micro-publishing is best described as a web service that allows subscribers to broadcast short messages to other subscribers of the service. These micro-posts can be made public on a website or distributed to a private group.

Subscribers read micro-blog posts online or request that updates be delivered in real time to their desktops as an instant message or sent to a mobile device as a text message. Twitter is the most prominent of these new applications.

The appeal of micro-blogging is both its immediacy and portability. Posts are brief (typically 140–200 characters) and can be written or received with a variety of computing devices, including cellphones. Although most micro-blog broadcasts are posted as text, some micro-blogging services allow video or audio posts to so-called mo-blogs, popularised by sites such as Tumblr.com and Posterous.com.

The mobile phone is becoming increasingly popular as a micro-blogging tool as 3G mobile phone technology allows for instant and fast blogging ability and is always easier to access than a computer. Couple this with mobile features specifically for sharing information and pictures on blogging sites that are now available on handsets, and the result is the speed and ease of use of micro-blogging being taken to new levels.

Traditional media organisations including *The New York Times* and the BBC are following suit and have begun to send headlines and links in micro-blog posts. Other potential applications of micro-blogging include traffic and sports updates and emergency broadcast systems – all very useful when updates are delivered to mobile handsets in particular.

But the most profound effects of this new instant broadcasting by citizens have been seen in the wake of political strife, when governments have cracked down on the media and tried to strangle the voice of the people. In Africa, news on the Kenyan and Zimbabwean election crises was broadcast to people around the world via Twitter, and recently the people of Iran gathered support for their cause from across the globe when they took to Twitter, combined with YouTube, to keep the world informed of their own election crisis. It is in these moments that social media show their true worth.

TREND SNACK

or so and deploy your own social network. Facebook's value lies in its ability to attract and retain an audience of more than 200 million connected users,[1] not to mention the precious data it gleans every time those users interact on or with the site.

These networks are made up of individuals – ordinary citizens if you will – who, whether they're aware of it or not, have evolved from passive consumers into active prosumers (simultaneous producers and consumers of content online).

The moment they register a free account with sites such as Flickr, YouTube, Zoopy, Twitter, Facebook and others, they cross the proverbial publishing Rubicon and begin to construct a social graph around themselves online. They upload photos, create videos, write blog posts and link to each other. The information highway has been replaced by a throbbing, thriving ecosystem powered by people who have never previously had the means or opportunity to publish. It has left long-established brands, and the custodians of those brands, reeling.

Why are marketers, advertisers and brand managers so intimidated by the idea of a digitally empowered, socially networked consumer? I think it has something to do with the generally accepted patterns and methods we've constructed around marketing over decades, spanning the industrial and information economies on which so many iconic brands have been built. I also think it has something to do with our obsession with the idea of what a 'brand' is and how much a 'brand' is worth.

Let's talk about that for a second. 'Brand' and corporate identity are not synonymous. And yet we spend fortunes with agencies that 'creatively' round the corners on our logo or change a few words in our tagline in the vain hope that it will somehow magically change consumers' perceptions of us.

Your logo – your corporate identity – is just that. Every consumer you engage with will have established a different set of associations, emotions, experiences and stories around that logo – and so no two consumers will feel the same. Some of those stories will be positive and some will be negative. I hear very few consumers complaining about the design of the logo of their bank of choice, but plenty complaining about the dodgy service they endured at the hands of an incompetent consultant or administrator.

Marketers cannot afford to spend money on channels simply because 'that's the way we've always done it'.

As *The Cluetrain Manifesto* says so well: 'A powerful global conversation has begun. Through the Internet people are discovering and inventing new ways to share relevant knowledge with blinding speed. As a direct result markets are getting smarter – and getting smarter faster than most companies.'[2]

It is not enough to come up with a 'big idea', split your spend across 'trusted media' – TV, radio, print, outdoor – and hope like hell the message sticks, nobody complains and the odd person buys something.

Ask yourself: do you ever change channels when adverts flight while you are watching your favourite sitcom or sports programme? Do you switch radio stations while some voiceover artist waffles on about another special insurance offering? How often do you commute on the highway? How many billboards and street-pole adverts do you pass on your way to work? Can you name them, remember them, or remember the last time one of them called you to action?

If you answered yes to the first two questions and no to the last, and you are a marketer or work in a company that uses any of those channels to speak to consumers, isn't that downright hypocritical?

Here's the bottom line. We have made the transition from the information age to an Attention Economy. Information, thanks to the sheer size of the web and the brilliance of Google, is freely available and widely distributed. Expertise is within everyone's reach.

So information isn't the problem – consumers have plenty of that; the problem is that the demands we place on consumers' attention spans simply exceed their capacity. Whether they're conscious of it or not, consumers are progressively inoculating themselves against marketing messages that are not absolutely relevant to them.

Marketers need not only understand these new platforms but also need to get their hands dirty using them.

This is no scarier than when mobile phones arrived in South Africa, or for that matter when email, or before that faxes, became a reality of the ever-changing communication landscape.

You cannot differentiate yourself on product or price any more. Companies that are authentic, transparent and engaging in this new 'Attention Economy' will rise above the competition.

An identity crisis: Open standards and data portability

There's no doubt that even in South Africa the social web is reaching truly widespread adoption, with our local radio stations punting their Twitter profiles, for example, and over 1 million people using Facebook. Despite this, the question remains: can these millions of social users take back control of their personal information? And on the flip side, what could researchers discover and application-developers create if they had access to the masses of social data currently spread throughout the web?

The realisation of just how much of our data we share and

relinquish when using Google's array of products, and social sites such as Facebook and YouTube, is staggering. Even more disturbing is that if we took the time to read the terms and conditions of using these sites we'd realise that they retain ownership of much of the content we create, our private data and our relationship dynamics.

Luckily, the building blocks that allow us to open up these closed walls of data exist right now: all that is missing is a strategy for putting it all together. Like that oft-quoted truism: you may not be interested in strategy, but strategy is interested in you.

The concern over privacy issues on the web, the need for users like you and I who have multiple online profiles and identities (not to mention about a hundred passwords across them all) is a major trend we should expect to see driving the evolution of the web in the next year or so.

The promise of Web 1.0 was the transfer of information across a network with a speed and efficiency previously unknown to humankind. The promise of Web 2.0 is the web evolving into a fully-fledged computing platform with a richer user experience focusing on collaboration and content creation. The promise of Web 3.0 or the so-called semantic web is the idea that the web will learn about you – the user – the more that you interact with it.

Put on your game face

The gaming industry has in the past few years shown considerable growth, even surpassing the movie industry. Titles such as *Halo 3* and *Grand Theft Auto IV* have brought new fans to the gaming world.

Despite the 'PC gaming is dead' sentiments expressed by many,[3] PC gaming is still alive and continues to get well-deserved

Twitter

Loren Phillips

Twitter started as a simple social network. People could create a free profile and begin updating their status in 140 characters or less – sharing everything with their 'followers' from what they ate for breakfast to how to bake the best banana bread.

Then something unexpected happened.

Twitter users took Twitter to the next level, developing ways to respond to each other and to tag their so-called tweets. Developers Biz Stone, Evan Williams and Jack Dorsey could hardly have imagined the way this medium would change the way we do things.

After the birth of Twitter, small start-ups and amateur coders quickly got on the bandwagon and dreamed up all sorts of third-party applications that would allow users to aggregate, analyse, filter, forward, reply to and track conversations that they were interested in.

The constant and connected real-time conversation had truly begun. According to TechCrunch, Twitter doubled its number of users in March 2009 alone to a staggering 9.3 million. Between June 2008 and June 2009 the number of unique visitors to Twitter.com increased by 1 928% to bring its total users to 21 million, earning Twitter its first appearance on comScore's list of the top 50 most-visited websites.

This hype was fuelled by celebrities such as Oprah who began using the service to engage with her fans, as did Britney Spears and Lance Armstrong. Ashton Kutcher became the first person to reach a million followers using his tweets to promote his new movies, share twitpics of his wife and talk about football. Of course, high-profile celebrities run the risk of imposters using their names to any end, but Twitter now offers verification for accounts like Kutcher's, which involves the website authenticating real celebrity profiles to discourage imposters and hijackers.

Businesses worldwide are realising the business applications inherent in this form of brief, instant, real-time communication and are starting to get on board. Twitter offers a vast pool of free sources to search, determine trends and influence and manage relationships. Being able to listen and respond to customers is in a brand's best interest. Not being part of the conversation

TREND SNACK

Twitter *continued*

can only lead to a widening disconnect between the brand and its user.

Starbucks in the USA has integrated Twitter into a multi-media ad campaign, and a bakery in Shoreditch in the UK tweets as soon as the bread comes out of the oven. Locally, Vida e Caffè has employed Twitter as a tool to engage directly with its customer base by listening and responding to any customer complaints and suggestions, giving out customer of the day awards and generally keeping followers in the loop about any new in-store developments.

Some of the more unexpected players also engaging in the conversation range from preachers to porn stars and super-savvy businesses – they are all experimenting with more quirky offerings. Methodist University Hospital in Memphis uses Twitter as a way of selling its services and promoting webcasting of various procedures, including brain surgery. On a more palatable note, Townhouse Hotel Maastricht in the Netherlands encourages guests to tweet their requests to the front desk.

The beauty of Twitter lies in its simplicity. Who would have thought that with just 140 characters Twitter would forever change the way that celebrities communicate with their fans and brands communicate with their customers.

T R E N D   S N A C K

attention from developers and many gamers. Still, there is no denying the significant move towards video game consoles. Microsoft's Xbox 360 (X360), Sony's PlayStation 3 (PS3) and Nintendo's Wii are the current favourites, with the latter being the most family-oriented.

Game consoles have also become capable home entertainment centres. The X360 and PS3 act as media players. With Xbox 360's Xbox Live (XBL) and through PlayStation Home services, subscribers can rent movies, download games, buy additional content for games and download updates, among other things.

One of the most exciting developments in console gaming has been in controllers. Cordless controllers have meant that it is not necessary to sit at a blinding distance from the screen and have at the same time afforded the player a certain amount of flexibility. Motion-sensing controllers, such as the Wii Remote (the Wiimote) make use of optical-sensor and accelerometer technology to detect movements made by the player to interact with the game. Microsoft recently revealed a gesture-based controlling system, called Project Natal for the X360.[4] In this case, there is no gadget that is the controller – the player's body is the controller.

As mobile phones get increasingly powerful (a combination of stronger processors and dedicated video accelerators), mobile games have gained complexity and visual appeal. Some developers have even taken the innovative move of incorporating phone functions into games. A good example is *The Journey*, where the cellphone towers or cells play a role in determining the character's movement. The opportunity to make use of location-based gaming on mobile is not yet fully explored but has massive potential.

Mobile gaming does not end with phones, of course; there are handhelds such as the Sony PlayStation Portable (PSP) and Nintendo DSi. The newly announced PSP go is even set to incorporate TV and video-on-demand.

Games may have been reserved for pimply teen geeks in the past but the audience has since broadened. The Wii is almost synonymous with family gaming with its easy-to-get-into games, such as *Wii Sports*. Nintendo has also successfully used gaming technology outside the gaming sphere. *Wii Fit*, for example, is an exercise programme that is carried out on a special controller, the Wii

Balance Board. There are several other applications of gaming technology that extend beyond entertainment; simulation programs in the military for jet pilots are a good example.

The rise in the number of people with Internet access has had implications in the gaming world. PC gamers have for many years enjoyed competitive networked gaming and in more recent years, the Massively Multiplayer Online Role-Playing Games (MMORPG) boom with games such as *World of Warcraft* has demonstrated the extent to which gaming can get social. Xbox Live has many other social aspects, from being able to play the same game with or against a friend or virtual stranger in another country altogether, to live chatting. Microsoft is also now integrating Twitter, Facebook and Last.fm.[5]

This move opens up the social sphere and brings together what are currently separate worlds for gamers. It fits with the current social media trend to combine the many identities a person may have on multiple services across the web, something like a FriendFeed.[6]

Another aspect of social gaming is sharing tips and tricks with other gamers. This is not new but video sharing websites such as YouTube have helped to advance how the gaming community communicates. Gamers typically upload walkthroughs (a recording of their games for others to serve as a guide), videos of their favourite game scenes, reviews and much more. This is a huge step from the oft-misinterpreted or otherwise 'dry' written word.

The success of Electronic Arts' (EA) *The Sims* shows that some people love to play dress-up. The controlling of simulated characters, which many base on their own lives, is really just a modern version of playing house. The Nintendo Wii lets you present yourself as a character called a Mii, which you can customise, while XBL has a similar avatar-based system which, it seems, it is planning to use a lot more of in future. One of Microsoft's many E3 2009 announce-ments is the introduction of virtual goods to XBL. It seems it will work just as in *Second Life* where you can spend real money on pre-mium items such as clothing for your avatar.

The South African online gaming experience has been some-what different from, for example, the UK and the USA. High band-width costs have meant that SA gamers have been denied services such as High Definition (HD) video rentals, downloading games which usually have huge file sizes, media streaming, and so on. The price of games, especially for consoles, is also quite hefty. It is no wonder that there is a growing market in trading games and im-porting them from online stores in other regions.

Facing the music

Perhaps no other industry is feeling the pressure of the changing digital landscape more than the music industry. Music fans have rather unashamedly expressed their disgust at the archaic approach of record companies – who have traditionally tied artists into wa-tertight contracts, forcing customers to enjoy music one way and one way only. They have responded by establishing formidable peer-to-peer file transfer networks on the web. These networks are responsible for terabytes of proprietary music and video, including the latest prime-time television series and Hollywood blockbusters, being shared openly and freely among millions of Internet users across the globe.

Few South African iPod owners even realise that they are effect-ively breaking the law when they rip their bought-and-owned CDs to iTunes to listen to on their iPods while at the gym or in the car.

iTunes and Amazon.com have not opened up their popular music stores to local markets, and as a result there is a growing frustration among local music lovers who simply have no legal way to enjoy the music they want, in the format they want. Local companies such as Pick 'n Pay and Musica have attempted to meet this need and failed dismally. The latest big brand to offer an online music store in South Africa is Nokia, but once again its music is encoded with Digital Rights Management (DRM) software and is not Apple-compatible, meaning Mac users are stymied. It's a good attempt, but still not quite there.

Notable international artists such as Trent Reznor of Nine Inch Nails, Radiohead, Dave Matthews and Madonna have realised the need for reinvention in their industry and have turned their focus to producing better live acts, making money off tours and merchandise as opposed to expecting the bulk of their revenue to come from record sales. Radiohead went as far as launching an entire album for free online, asking fans to pay only what they thought the album was worth. Expect South African artists, record companies and music fans to ride this trend over the next few years.

As a trendspotter, watch the music industry and its happenings closely in the next few years to gain valuable insights into how digital technology and the connectedness it brings will impact on big business.

Notes

1 Michael Arrington, 'Facebook Now Nearly Twice the Size of MySpace Worldwide'. TechCrunch, January 2009, www.techcrunch.com/2009/01/22/facebook-now-nearly-twice-the-size-of-myspace-worldwide/ (accessed 1 July 2009).

2 Rick Levine, Christopher Locke, Doc Searls and David Weinberger, *The Cluetrain Manifesto: The End of Business as Usual* (Perseus Publishing, 2000). This book is also available online at www.cluetrain.com (accessed 1 July 2009).

3 Tom Orry, 'PC Gaming is Dead'. Videogamer.com, 18 December 2007, www.
   videogamer.com/features/article/18-12-2007-223.html (accessed 1 July 2009).
   This is one of many articles expressing this view.
4 For more about Project Natal, see www.xbox.com/en-US/live/projectnatal/
   (accessed 1 July 2009).
5 Last.fm is '[t]he world's largest online music catalogue, with free music streaming,
   videos, pictures, lyrics, charts, artist biographies, concerts and Internet radio'. See
   www.last.fm (accessed 1 July 2009).
6 FriendFeed allows you to build a customised feed that consolidates content that
   has been shared with you and that you want to share with others.

FLUX OBSERVATION

How technology affects your child's mind

Carina Louw

A SCI-FI future is upon us – a new generation has been born and bred in a world of accelerated technological innovation. As the age at which children start to become familiar with computers gets ever-lower, there grows a technological divide between parents and their digital native children.

Parents are increasingly concerned that by allowing their children to use cellphones or computers, they are exposing them to a digital world infested with hidden dangers. While many parents know about dangers such as cyber bullying and sexual predators, new evidence suggests that the amount of time their children are spending on-line, thumb-wrestling with a phone or playing with gaming consoles erodes literacy skills and general knowledge, wrecks attention spans and lessens healthy social interaction. The question is: are we raising the most socially inept and dumbest generation yet?

Identity and social interaction

As the first generation to grow up technologically fluent, today's tweens and teens are flocking to be part of social networks as a way to establish their social identities.

California-based neuroscientist Dr Gary Small, who specialises in brain functioning, explains that young minds are more suscep-tible to on-screen influences. Teenage years are an important, yet turbulent period of identity formation and role development in which adolescents are intensely focused on social life. During these years, empathy skills (situated in the temporal lobe) and complex reasoning skills (in the frontal lobe) are not yet fully developed.[1] This explains why teens are predisposed to being self-centred and sometimes display an inability to put themselves in someone else's shoes, aspects they grow out of over time through social interaction.

Brain scientists now believe that overexposure to interactive technologies from a young age may suppress frontal-lobe executive skills, stifle the ability to communicate face to face and consequently stunt the maturation process – ultimately freezing the brain in a teen-brain state. This evokes a chilling thought about how social networks are interfering with normal growth patterns.

Being able to share photographs instantly and post regular updates of their every thought or action is believed to induce an addiction to instant gratification and sensationalism, ultimately creating the potential for a generation of self-centred young people with an unstable sense of their own identities.

Moreover, because they are not speaking to people face to face, but rather online, it makes it easier to reveal themselves in a way that they might not have been comfortable with in a real-world situation. People become less conscious of how they come across to other people in an online context and feel less inhibited, almost like an alcohol-induced self-confidence.

British Professor Susan Greenfield recently warned that children raised on virtual interactions may well start to see it as the norm:

> *Real conversation in real time may eventually give way to these sanitized and easier screen dialogues, in much the same way as killing, skinning and butchering an animal to eat has*

been replaced by the convenience of packages of meat on the supermarket shelf. Perhaps future generations will recoil with similar horror at the messiness, unpredictability and immediate personal involvement of a three-dimensional, real-time interaction.[2]

Kids need real-life human interaction to teach them fundamental social skills, such as interpreting facial expressions and other non-verbal messages during a conversation.

Constant distractions

A study by the American Kaiser Family Foundation found that young people absorb an average of 8.5 hours of digital and video sensory stimulation per day and some are sending and receiving as many as 80 text messages during that time. By the age of twenty, the average teen has spent an estimated 20 000 hours on the web, and over 10 000 hours playing video games.[3]

Attention spans and concentration are being stretched thin by the many competing interactive technologies and children have come to expect constant stimulation to ward off boredom.

In his book Gary Small reports that web-surfing, multi-tasking, and information overload can accelerate learning and creativity, but warns that they may also increase Attention Deficit Disorder (ADD). Besides making people less efficient (which can lead to errors) through constant distractions, rapidly alternating between tasks has other unforeseen side effects:

When paying partial continuous attention, people may place their brains in a heightened state of stress. They no longer have time to reflect, contemplate or make thoughtful decisions. They exist in a sense of constant crisis – on alert for a new contact or bit of exciting news or information at any moment.[4]

But the news is not all bad. What is quite unique to this generation is that because they grew up in a world where they are constantly bombarded with information, it has made their young brains more adroit at filtering information and making quick decisions.

Canadian professor Don Tapscott, author of *Grown up Digital: How the Net Generation is Changing your World*, explains that from ages eight to eighteen, when the brain is still developing, children's brains are being hard-wired to live in a digital culture. In other words, technology is literally rewiring their brains to adapt to a new multi-tasking culture.[5]

Rewiring the brain

Neurological studies show that learning to read changes the brain's circuitry by forging new connections. Scientists hypothesise that reading on the Internet is also affecting the brain's hard-wiring in a way that is different from book reading.

On paper, text has a fixed beginning, middle and end, where readers focus for a sustained period on one author's vision. Online readers jump from one link to the next, often forgetting where they started, just to go back to the beginning and be sent off in another direction. In a digital world, readers compose their own beginnings, middles and endings, and frequently do not simply read one author's opinion but comments and input from various contributors. This shifts thinking from linear thought to non-linear, networked thought. New forms of reading are emerging as users 'power browse' horizontally through numerous websites going for quick wins instead of perusing material vertically.

As adults, we worry about the impact of technology on our own ability to think deeply and critically. But if kids are growing up with information served to them in this scattered online format, can they learn to be good critical thinkers? Tapscott argues that kids are actually better analytical thinkers than their parents who grew up passively watching TV. Television is a one-way conversation with one end receiving information passively, whereas the online world invites input, allows for changes and offers a cornucopia of opinions.

Small also did research on how technology has altered the way young minds develop, function and interpret information. He tested Internet-savvy brains against older individuals who have never searched for content online before. The Magnetic Resonance Imaging (MRI) results showed that both book reading and Internet searching stimulated the regions of the brain controlling language, memory and vision in both tech-savvy and tech-disabled brains. But what is surprising, is that the Internet search lit up more areas of the net-savvy brain, additionally activating the regions controlling complex reasoning and decision-making.

The increased brain activity, most likely due to the multiple quick choices that an online search involves, suggests that subjects experienced a richer sensory experience and heightened attention.

Small's findings are provocative since they indicate that routine online searching helps stimulate and possibly improve brain function, effectively debunking the myth that children are becoming less intelligent.

The kids are all right

History is riddled with examples of how each significant communication revolution within society brought with it fears and sceptics. More than 2 000 years ago, both Socrates and Plato warned about a different kind of information development – the rise of the written word. They feared that as people came to rely on writing as a substitute for knowledge it would inevitable damage human thinking and memory.

Similar opinions were voiced with the arrival of the printing press in the 15th century. In both cases the arguments made by the doomsayers were spot on – both printing and the written word, which necessitated that people learn how to read, shifted society's thinking and brought about remarkable change. However, at that time, the sceptics couldn't foresee how writing, printing and reading would serve to spread information and ideas across the world, spark innovation and expand human knowledge.

The difference, in the case of the digital communications revolution, is the unprecedented pace and rate of change. It is creating what Small calls a 'brain gap' between young and old that is being forged in a single generation. 'Perhaps not since early man first discovered how to use a tool has the human brain been affected so quickly and so dramatically.'

Instead of the traditional generation gap, we are witnessing the beginning of a brain gap that separates digital natives, born into 24/7 technology and the older generation, their parents, who came to computers and other digital technology as adults. The Internet is not simply changing the way people live but altering the way minds work. Small calls it an 'evolutionary change' that will position the technologically fluent at the top of a new social order.

Weighing the benefits

Embrace technology as an educational tool

The dangers and risks posed by technology are real, but should not overshadow the huge benefits it can bring to children and young people. Because video games are a significant part of the entertainment landscape for a majority of teens (and many adults) they are increasingly being viewed as promising educational tools.

Research has found that surgeons who regularly play video games make fewer errors in the operating theatre because playing increases hand–eye coordination, peripheral vision and reaction time.

The common perception that the most popular types of games are filled with violence is incorrect. They are, in fact, games that involve racing and role-playing, puzzles and sports. These games often require a level of problem-solving, overcoming obstacles and achieving goals – skills that educators usually applaud. Plus, with Wii gaming consoles, gaming has become an interactive hobby that can get kids off the couch and involve the whole family.

It is of utmost importance to teach children how to work on the Internet and with computers. It is not about showing them how to use PowerPoint or create a podcast but rather about teaching them how to use and interpret information from the Internet in a way that will allow them to develop their own ideas.

It is important for them to learn such fundamental cognitive abilities as the capacity to think critically and logically, to analyse an argument, to learn and remember information and, most importantly, to distinguish fact from opinion. A realistic balance between reading books in printed form and reading online is crucial.

Training for future jobs

Some literacy experts say that online reading skills will help children fare better when they begin looking for digital-age jobs. Future and current jobs will require transferable thinking skills more than content knowledge or task-specific skills. Children should be equipped to learn new things since accelerating technological change is swiftly generating the need for new skills and knowledge.

The teamwork involved in games such as *World of Warcraft* is considered by some cultural commentators to be excellent training.[6] *WoW,* as its 10 million fans worldwide call it, requires that each player via his or her online avatar complete numerous quests individually or as part of a team. The leader of a team is selected not by credentials but based on how much he or she contributes to the success of a team. The game is teaching young people to operate as part of a team and constantly to stay focused on resolving unexpected problems.

Moreover, it is estimated that almost half of the world's bloggers are still in their teens. Younger users are the most avid content creators, and most post their content online to express themselves creatively and to share their experiences with others. This generation cannot be defined as passive and, unlike older generations, they do not just observe, they constantly participate.

In the online world they can debate, argue, play, critique, investigate, invent, seek and inform. Interactive technologies are, in fact, training them to become highly networked and teaching them the valuable skills they'll need to use in social settings and at work in non-traditional career settings in the digital age.

Sharing with your kids is caring

As mentioned, there are some grounds for concern and parents should not be complacent about these. It is important to understand how technology is affecting young lives and brains and to try to manage this. Some ground rules include:

❑ *Technology should never be used as a virtual nanny.* Children should be educated to use technology as a tool from an early age and not be left to their own devices. Especially with young children, rather have a computer in the living room than in their bedrooms;

❑ *Engage, share and learn about technology with your child.* This can nullify the numerous threats posed by technology;

❑ *Teach children the value of personal privacy.* Include lessons on what is appropriate to post and communicate on the Internet. One of the biggest concerns for critics is young people's lack of regard for online privacy. A growing number of job-seekers are learning that lesson the hard way as photos taken at alcohol-fuelled parties have been discovered by employers who are poking around Facebook and MySpace for clues about the character of potential employees. Plus what is posted online in an impulsive moment can end up circulating in virtual space for years to come. Instruct your children on how to put their profile on a privacy setting because an alarming number of teens do not even consider doing this; and

❑ *Set realistic boundaries when it comes to when, where and how technology is used.* For example, taking away a cellphone from a teenager whose life revolves around communication will be more damaging than the hours he or she spends on MXit.

Balance has never been more important. Children need to learn human contact skills and nurture real relationships with people before having 800 friends on Facebook. It also means making the effort to cut back on time spent with technology – plan a family dinner, take your children for a walk and take time out with them to define new priorities.

Children born after 1990 have no recollection of what life was like before technology invaded every part of our lives. They were born and bred on a diet of constantly flickering images emanating from computer and TV screens, have had generous helpings of video games, digital music players and cellphones and have been force-fed infotainment from the word go. As a consequence, they are being hard-wired to live, operate, socialise and think differently from their predecessors. But digitally native children may be acquiring a new form of intelligence that their grandparents and even parents could never have dreamed of. Today's technologies are supplying them with incredible tools, which if used with a good measure of balance, could potentially make them one of the smartest generations ever.

Notes and references

1 Gary Small, *iBrain: Surviving the Technological Alteration of the Modern Mind* (HarperCollins, 2008).

2 Greenfield is cited in Patrick Wintour, 'Facebook and Bebo Risk "Infantilizing" the Human Mind.' Guardian Online, 24 February 2009, www.guardian.co.uk/uk/2009/feb/24/social-networking-site-changing-childrens-brains (accessed 7 May 2009).

3 Kaiser Family Foundation, 'Generation M: Media in the Lives of 8–18 Year-olds – Report'. The Henry Kaiser Family Foundation Online, 9 March 2005, www.kff.org/entmedia/7251.cfm (accessed 7 May 2009).

4 Small, *iBrain*.

5 Don Tapscott, *Grown up Digital: How the Net Generation is Changing your World* (McGraw Hill, 2008).

6   Executive Vice President of Fedex, Rob Carter, talks about how *World of Warcraft* contributes to a form of training for future jobs in Anne Fisher, 'When Gen X Runs the Show'. Times Online, 25 May 2009, www.time.com/time/specials/packages/article/0,28804,1898024_1898023_1898086,00.html (accessed 28 May 2009).

Anne Fisher, 'When Gen X Runs the Show'. Times Online, 25 May 2009, www.time.com/time/specials/packages/article/0,28804,1898024_1898023_1898086,00.html (accessed 28 May 2009).

Amanda Lenhart, 'Teens, Video Games and Civics: What the Research is Telling us'. Pew Internet and American Life Project, 2 November 2008, www.pewinternet.org/Presentations/2008/Teens-Video-Games-and-Civics.aspx (accessed 9 June 2009).

Malcolm Ritter, 'Scientists Question Technology's Effect on Social Development'. Missourian Online, 3 December 2008, www.columbiamissourian.com/stories/2008/12/03/scientists-ask-technology-rewiring-our-brains/ (accessed 7 May 2009).

Daniel Sieberg, 'Are Video Games Actually Good for Kids?' CBS News Online, 16September 2008, www.cbsnews.com/stories/2008/09/16/eveningnews/eyeontech/main4453801.shtml (accessed 9 June 2009).

Maryanne Wolf, *Proust and the Squid: The Story and Science of the Reading Brain* (Harper Perennial, 2008).

The impact of the
2010 FIFA Soccer World Cup

What will the world cup really mean for South Africa?

Gary Bailey

Gary Bailey is crazy about football. He is a former goalkeeper for Manchester United (373 appearances), Kaizer Chiefs and England, and has been to the world cup as both a player (in 1986 with England) and as a TV commentator (Germany, 2006). He was an ambassador for South Africa's 2010 world cup bid. He currently works for SuperSport TV (and has done for the past twenty years) as a guest and presenter. For the past three years he has given presentations on the business opportunities related to the world cup to companies around southern Africa (www.GamePlan2010.com). Besides his vast football qualifications and experience, he also holds a Bachelor of Sciences (B.Sc.) in Physics and an MBA from Henley in Oxford.

DID YOU honestly believe that the Confederations Cup was going to be such a success? Most people I chatted to didn't and there were certainly plenty of doubters abroad. But we hosted a wonderful event and the world responded positively. Visitors and spectators embraced our culture of *vuvuzelas* (well, most did) and they loved our happy dancing crowds, the efficient organisation (aside from a few transport issues) and excellent performances by Bafana Bafana. But the Confed Cup was only a warm up for an event that shadows it by comparison. While very few visitors arrived to enjoy the Confed Cup, the 2010 FIFA World Cup, by contrast, will bring more fans to our shores than we have ever seen, or are likely ever to see again.

If you think that the 2010 FIFA World Cup is only about four weeks of soccer, think again.

Now that the 2009 general elections are well behind us, a strong trend of nation-building has emerged, and the world cup is perfectly timed to contribute to this objective. South Africans are likely to experience once more the unity that hasn't been felt since the Rugby World Cup in 1995. Aside from the positive nation-building effects this event will have, the excitement of seeing so many superstars in our country, of witnessing huge crowds of soccer fans at both the stadiums and fan parks, and of being at the centre of the world's attention for four whole weeks, is building – now this is a dream unimaginable twenty years ago in South Africa.

The big picture

Leading up to 2010, the government has committed to massive infrastructural investment of R17.4 billion, and during 2010 visitors are expected to spend over R15 billion – with foreign visitors estimated to spend R8.5 billion of that according to auditors Grant Thornton.[1]

The Department of Tourism estimates that the South African economy will benefit substantially from the world cup, which is an enormous bonus in recessionary times. With an estimated 1 billion people watching the final alone, and an estimated 500 million viewers per world cup game,[2] South Africa should see a significant increase in all types of tourism after the event.

This is wonderful news for the country, coming at a time when the general confidence of most people has taken a big dip due to the credit crunch. In fact, economists reckon that our recession will be one of the shortest in the world due to two factors: the Credit Act, which limited the effects of the credit crunch; and the arrival of the biggest sporting event in the world.

Around 204 countries enter the competition and 32 teams qualify to play in the world cup. Fans from 31 countries will therefore be drawn to South Africa. It is estimated that the world cup will bring close to 200 000 long-haul or overseas visitors to our shores, with another 180 000 coming from Africa. That is more than fifteen times the number of tourists who came to South Africa for the Rugby World Cup, our biggest single event to date.

Anyone in business will tell you that a 10% or 15% increase in the demands placed on the daily running of a business results in intense pressure. Now double that and keep doubling. Taking into account everyone involved – spectators, officials, media, sponsors and, of course, the players themselves – the event starting on 11 June, running until 11 July 2010, will bring a huge demand for products and services, ranging from food to transport, security to accommodation and even language translation.[3]

More important than the financial benefits, is the opportunity to rebrand a country. The Germans used the 2006 FIFA World Cup to their advantage, successfully portraying their country to the world as a fun-loving, friendly place, qualities that few had previously associated with Germany.

A successful world cup will contribute immensely towards rebranding South Africa as a safe, world-class country, altering the prevalent Afro-pessimistic view of Africa in the process. Imagine what this can do for us and for our tourism industry?

On the road

With only a few months to go until kick-off at Soccer City on 11 June 2010, we are up to speed with construction in spite of the strikes (that are now fully resolved) and the bad press overseas that has raised concerns over the readiness of our stadiums. In Cape Town and Durban, we have built two of the most stunning stadiums the world has ever seen. The facilities and the settings are world-class; the Green Point Stadium has Table Mountain on one side and the Waterfront and Robben Island on the other – an unrivalled location.

Locals have been most concerned about the performance of our national team, Bafana Bafana, but during the Confederations Cup the team was superb, taking the number one (Brazil) and number two (Spain) teams right down to the wire. However, host-country teams in previous world cups have always benefited from having

The changing nature of celebrity culture

Dion Chang

The name Susan Boyle didn't mean a thing to anyone until she auditioned for the reality TV show *Britain's Got Talent*. Middle-aged, frumpy and unpolished, her appearance on stage was greeted with derision. The live studio audience laughed and sneered at her, assuming her attempt to compete on such a platform was brazen and doomed to failure.

In a celebrity-obsessed world where youth is worshipped, size zero is seen as a natural benchmark and models – who actually fit those requirements – are further airbrushed and Photoshopped to perfection, Susan Boyle was the joker of the pack. That is, until she opened her mouth to sing.

She not only floored the judges and sceptical audience, but became the YouTube phenomenon of 2009. She didn't win the competition but then she didn't have to. Her video clip was viewed more than 100 million times and she was interviewed by the likes of Oprah Winfrey and Larry King, providing her with a global following. Susan Boyle was a watershed moment in 21st-century celebrity culture.

Not so long ago, Paris Hilton represented the epitome of celebrity culture, as well as everything that was wrong with it. She was famous for being famous and blazed a trail for a slew of F-grade celebrities who elbowed their way into the spotlight using the same claim to fame. Reality TV shows, such as *Big Brother*, were responsible for unleashing these vacuous personalities on an unsuspecting world.

But the tide is turning and it is no coincidence that the reality TV shows that remain popular are those that require real skill and talent. This shift matches the changing mood of the world.

As more and more people strive for and demand authenticity, so too does our benchmark shift of who or what constitutes a role model. At the moment, sports stars are the new heroes and with the prospect of the 2010 FIFA World Cup, soccer players in particular are the focus. Hollywood stars may still dominate the glossy magazine covers but it is the soccer players who are not only bagging the big endorsement deals but also dominating the gossip columns – a sure sign of celebrity status.

In business terms, Cristiano Ronaldo's transfer from Manchester United to Real Madrid for

T R E N D   S N A C K

The changing nature of celebrity culture *continued*

an unprecedented £80 million was the largest-ever deal in soccer history, and a crowd of 80 000 fans turned out just to see him don the Real Madrid jersey. Similarly, the unveiling of David Beckham's underwear campaign for Armani at Selfridges in London nearly caused a riot. One could say that there has always been a tripartite alliance between sport, fashion and business, but as 2010 beckons this trend will accelerate and the designer brands are already scrabbling for territory.

Aside from using Beckham for his underwear campaigns, Armani also supplies Chelsea Football Club with its off-field kit and created an Armani lounge for the Stamford Bridge Stadium. Dolce&Gabbana dresses the Italian national soccer team while Paul Smith nabbed the contract to dress Manchester United.

Not only are soccer stars fit, healthy and easy on the eye – making them ideal models – but their global fan bases make global brand association a breeze. Manchester United fans alone number over 330 million, while the audience of the FIFA World Cup easily outstrips both the Cricket and Rugby World Cups, and even surpasses global audiences for the Olympic Games.

And we haven't even begun to factor in the female (and gay male) audiences who really have no interest in the game whatsoever …

T R E N D S N A C K

the home fans cheer them on, and even if Bafana don't get past the first round, I don't think it's a real problem. Both hosts of the 2008 European Championship, Austria and Switzerland, fell at the first-round hurdle, and yet the tournament was a great success.

What does it mean for you?

The four weeks of the world cup are going to impact on our lives whether we like it or not. With an influx of tourists, life will not be the same – even getting home from work will be tricky as buses full of fans going to and from stadiums and fan parks will cause congestion. One positive is that all the schools will be closed, so there is an opportunity to rent out your house and head for the hills.

But bear in mind that due to the influx of visitors, finding holiday accommodation without booking in advance will be difficult. If you are planning to go on a quiet, family holiday, try to avoid the nine host cities and book early. It will be difficult to get a flight, car rental or hotel room unless you book in advance, or plan your holiday before or after the event instead.

If you don't manage to get tickets to the games, don't stress. The fan parks and public viewing areas will be magical places to watch the games alongside thousands of fans – in fact, many people in Germany preferred to watch at the fan parks. Over 500 000 fans turned up to the game between Germany and Poland in Berlin. What a sight that was, and what an atmosphere. The reason why so many fans in Germany preferred to watch the matches at the fan parks was because of the vibe, like a massive party, and the amount of space that was available.

Business opportunities

So what is up for up for grabs during this event from a business perspective? With the world cup being so much bigger than any other event that South Africa has hosted to date, it is doubtful whether existing resources such as skills and service provision will be sufficient to cope with demand. For example, Germany brought in 22 000 extra chefs and 880 000 extra chairs. Admittedly, our world cup will not be as big as Germany's, but even if we need to import 20 000 chairs, who is going to do it?

Some sponsors are paying as much as US$250 million to be involved in the event – and it is likely that they will spend many more millions to leverage their exposure – think of top-class food and drink, quality chefs, tablecloths, chairs, tables, ovens, fridges, etc., and begin imagining where your company might fit into the picture.

Activities and tourism

Fans will watch their teams play every three or four days. In the down-time in between matches, they will want to be kept busy. In Germany two of the more popular activities were five-a-side football and sightseeing.

The good thing about five-a-side football is that it allows fans to sweat out the excesses of the previous night in a healthy, non-destructive manner. Setting up and running a five-a-side event is a simple way to generate money for your child's school or football club.

Fans will flock to local tourist spots. Tourist trips to historical sites and wildlife areas will be in great demand, generating healthy income for tourist operators. When matches are played in places such as Nelspruit (or any city with limited accommodation), fans won't want to travel back to the cities where they will be based during the tournament, such as Johannesburg, after the games (evening matches will only finish at about 11 p.m.). Instead, they may be enticed to stay at resorts on the outskirts of these towns. These fans would wake up in a relaxed setting, enjoy a bush walk, take in a few cultural activities or go horse riding before making their way back to Jo'burg in a leisurely manner.

Retail

Retail sales should spike during the world cup. Sales of clothing and official 2010 FIFA-branded items will sell most strongly, followed by tourist souvenirs and curios.

Accommodation

Another way to make money is through the provision of accommodation. I, for one, will rent out my house, along with a car and an attendant housekeeper. Property company Seeff has a website focused on assisting South Africans with renting their houses during the world cup. This includes taking deposits, ensuring the house is looked after, and collecting the money. All you would need to do is find a place to stay (this might be the perfect time to become friendly with the in-laws again).

While schools and universities are closed, it is also an opportunity to take the kids with you, returning home to a nice pile of cash.

Eating out

Eating out will be a different experience during the world cup. Opening hours will be extended to the early hours of the morning to cater for the needs of the fans, and there will be increased numbers of customers on game days. Consequently, it would make sense to keep menus simple to meet the increased demand.

Food, entertainers, TV screens, waiters, chefs, dancers and organisers will be in great demand.

Services

Most cleaning companies will be fully employed, ensuring that stadiums, fan parks, city centres, parks and beaches are presentable on a daily basis. This is non-negotiable due to the 'beautification' clause in the FIFA contracts signed by each host city. The sale of cleaning goods, detergents, etc. should see a huge increase as hotels, bed and breakfasts and lodges are inundated with customers.

With sponsors spending such large amounts to ensure that they benefit from their investments in the tournament, there will be a demand for companies and individuals to coordinate and ensure that marketing materials are distributed, and that the brands of the sponsors are visible. This includes putting up posters, waving flags, handing out flyers and leaflets, and ensuring that sponsors are noticed and enjoy a strong association with the event.

Transport

The transport industry will come under serious strain. During the world cup in Germany, millions of additional people used trains. South Africa is purchasing many new large buses to move football fans around. Roads will be congested, especially in the afternoons (when games are being played and rush-hour traffic is at its worst). There may be an opportunity to become a temporary taxi driver – the lady who picked me up from the airport in Munich two-and-half years ago was the mother of two young children who was making some extra money as a taxi driver during the event.

VIPs will also need transport, requiring chauffer-driven limos to take them around.

Think about transport companies renting their friends' and colleagues' fancy cars out during the event. These companies will need to hire more drivers and are likely to make a killing. So, get that lazy 21-year-old son off the couch and clean up the second car to use while your son chauffeurs tourists around in your fancy Mercedes, and take a cut of the profits!

Another sought after form of transportation will be flights and the attendant pilots and fuel. Huge demand is expected for private jets to whisk CEOs from game to game, and it's a need that we are going to battle to meet.

Insurance

Think about insurance needs – insurance against lost goods, illness, HIV/AIDS, crime … and that's just the beginning. There will also be a greater chance of damage or loss caused by large crowds arriving at or leaving stadiums and fan parks.. Imagine also the remote possibility of a footballer worth £30 million (about R450 million) slipping and breaking his leg in your establishment. You don't want to face occurrences such as these without insurance cover.

Security

One of the biggest demands will be for security personnel to safeguard the VIPs and media who will descend on South Africa, most of whom will be based in Johannesburg, where crime is a major concern.

Team-building

Many South African companies are seeing the world cup as a great opportunity to build team spirit within their organisations – to take workers in groups to watch the games and to provide TVs or radio commentary in the workplace so that staff can enjoy the events, with the aim of improving performance levels.

Networking

There will be plenty of opportunities for businesses and organisations to network with other companies from abroad; more companies and organisations need to become aware of the significant opportunities that will arise from the world cup. Previously, if you sent emails to prospective international clients, the chances were good that you would have received few replies, but try it now, mentioning that South Africa is hosting the FIFA 2010 Soccer World Cup and that if they visit you will host them or assist them in planning their trip. You might find your inbox suddenly clogged up with responses – how can any business with an international outlook pass up such an opportunity?

Reaching out

Try to leave a corporate-responsibility legacy by trying to source uniquely South African gifts and products from poor communities. This is no time to be shy. Make a noise about corporate South Africa being aware of the needs of the poor. Another method to raise money for your child's school, local church, or a poor local community, is to set up a Public Viewing Site. These are similar to fan parks, with screens to watch the games, but they differ in that branding is not allowed (for an official fan park you need permission from FIFA). So how will you make money with a Public Viewing Site? From the sale of food and drinks. Let's say you pay R1 000 to get a big screen in your local school hall, and you make R2 000 per game from the sale of food and drink; with three games per day your income will be R6 000, your costs R1 000, and your net profit R5 000.

Branding: A cautionary note

Branding is an issue that companies need to be aware of. At FIFA's insistence South Africa has introduced some of the strongest ambush marketing laws in the world. This means that unless you are an official sponsor you may not use any of the FIFA or host city logos, or any logos in any way associated with the event. Furthermore, you can't even use two items that describe the world cup. For example, my presentation on the 2010 FIFA World Cup is called GamePlan2010 – it used to be shown against a background of the South African flag until FIFA contacted me and said that putting 2010 and the flag together was a breach. If I didn't change it, legal action would follow. I have since removed the flag on my GamePlan2010 logo.

After the final whistle

Having made a small fortune during the world cup, what are the long-term benefits? If there is one lasting legacy that will benefit South Africa more than any other, it's an improvement in our crime-fighting ability. FIFA has insisted that central government and each host city sign contracts guaranteeing all visitors to South Africa absolute safety during their stay. With that in mind, there will be an extra R10 billion spent on improving crime fighting – 60 000 CCTV cameras will be installed in host cities, improved police training has been scheduled, and an extra 35 000 police will be recruited. My hope is that we can keep similar standards after the world cup. Imagine how tourism will increase if all of the nine host cities are perceived as safe tourist destinations.

An issue that will continue to be contested after the world cup is the status of sex workers. A reported 40 000 'ladies of the night' plied their trade in Germany during the four weeks of that country's world cup. HIV/AIDS is a huge problem in South Africa and, currently, sex work is illegal. In order to lessen health risks by regulating the industry, the government is considering legalising sex work, either for the duration of the tournament only, or on a permanent basis. This is both a moral and ethical issue that the government should perhaps consider asking South Africans to voice their opinions on through referendums or public discussions after the world cup.

After the world cup, the real benefits of the tournament will become evident – a much-improved road system; new, upgraded airports; world-class stadiums for future events; a substantial growth in tourism, especially in Cape Town, Port Elizabeth, Durban and Nelspruit; and a much-improved perception of South Africa as a safe, well-organised country.

You don't have to look too far ahead to find the good news in this.

Notes

1 Grant Thornton, 'Business of 2010'. See www.zoopy.com/search/2kf (accessed 20 July 2009).

2 See 'World Cup 2010 Info', www.cup2010.info/broadcasting/TVrights/TVrights. html (accessed 20 July 2009).

3 Marthinus van Schalkwyk, 'National 2010 FIFA World Cup Tournament Accommodation Workshop'. Polity.co.za, 12 October, 2006, www.polity. org.za/article/van-schalkwyk-national-2010-fifa-world-cup-tournament-accommodation-workshop-12102006-2006-10-12 (accessed 3 July 2009).

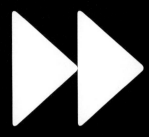

Living on fast forward

What's entertaining when we all have ADD?

Randall Abrahams

Randall Abrahams has spent his life listening to, watching, reading about and being enthralled by popular culture. He was the Station Manager at Good Hope FM in Cape Town in the mid-1990s before moving to Johannesburg where he helped establish the youth radio station YFM as an important new player in the commercial market. From 2002–06 he was the General Manager of Commercial Radio at the SABC, responsible for the successes of 5FM, Metro FM and Good Hope FM. Having recently completed judging his fifth season of the highly rated M-Net reality show *Idols*, Abrahams will also shortly feature on *SA's Got Talent* on SABC2. Abrahams has worked at the highest level in the broadcasting industry, spent time with its most talented individuals and seen his hero, Bruce Springsteen, on every tour since The Boss reformed the legendary E Street Band in 2000. He counts himself very lucky.

SO I watch a lot of pop culture and listen to a lot of music. By that, I mean that I engage with pop culture and music. I read magazines; I listen to the radio. I buy LPs. I watch music video channels; I search for clips on YouTube. I'm in 'a state of alert and continuous attention'.

Record company people probably dread my emails because I'm always asking about something that hasn't been released yet or that they don't have rights to (my humble apologies – Duncan G., Duncan S., Karl, Natasha, Steve).

I'd love to make a music video. I'd also like to write a No.1 hit that becomes a classic. I'll never reach the heights of 'You've Lost that Lovin' Feelin''(no one will) so I'll settle for 'Yesterday'.

Remember music videos. They bolstered the entire industry during the 1980s. *Thriller*, the album, has sold 50 million copies worldwide and counting.[1] Madonna became a star, Peter Gabriel made you forget that he was ever in Genesis, even a rock 'n roll throwback like The Boss made videos. And, no doubt, critics will argue that Duran Duran built a hit machine based on nothing more than sexy-dirty elegantly wasted shots of the band – 'Rio', 'Girls on Film', 'Wild Boys'.

I was thinking of a video shot using only one camera though, maybe two. Like Sinéad O'Connor crying a lonely forgotten tear on Prince's 'Nothing Compares 2 U'. I'm not too sure if I'd shoot in hi-def? It might not be a bad idea, but I wouldn't send the star to *Dr 90210* if she possessed a slight blemish on the left cheek. It would be like hi-def vérité.

No storyline; just pure performance. With only two cameras I wouldn't have much need for editing. Screenshots would last for more than a few seconds and I'd (hopefully) capture the *essence* of the performer. Kinda like The Stones at Altamont, or Hendrix at Monterey, or James Brown at the Boston Garden. Wow! It could be 'awesome'. One singer or performer, two cameras, sweat, purpose and attitude – reality rock 'n roll.

I would need a performer, right?

I'd need a damn fine performer. Someone 'road-tested'. Not one of these stage school kids who sing and dance like puppets.

Everyone would watch my video. What a revelation! Artist, camera, magic! I'm running away with myself here. I'm off to Cash Converters to buy a camera. I have friends at production companies – I must call them. My video infamy awaits …

It wasn't that long ago (all right, maybe about a century) that Al Jolson mouthed the first words on a motion picture screen. Those words found their way to collective ears and pierced the collective consciousness.

I read that the 'screen' is a two-way device. The audience may focus towards it but it has two sides. Movies reflect society. We watch something about ourselves and then we act out the next part.

Al Jolson performed a song. So did Bing, Frank, Elvis, The Beatles and Hendrix. Dylan made an interesting video with cue cards and Alan Ginsberg in attendance. Springsteen didn't want to make videos aside from recordings of his live performances. But in order to merge the MTV audience with the radio listener, pressing them to buy his singles and albums, he mimed to both 'Born in the USA' (badly) and 'Dancing in the Dark'. Furthermore, he played a character in a 'story' video for 'I'm on Fire'. So the song was being 'acted out' rather than executed. Do they make 'live' music videos any more?

These musical vignettes were instruments for promoting the sale of a product. It worked, and how. Kids dressed and danced like Michael Jackson. Where do you think would-be rappers learned those arcane finger signs from? But the MTV generation didn't last. Like punk in the wake of glam, grunge spat in the face of Reagan-friendly commoditised radio hits. Wow! This is like a damn history lesson. Even I'm impressed.

Where was I? Oh, music videos. They're so frenetic. Camera angles, colourations, dance moves, storylines, fast cuts, hairstyles. It's like *Gone with the Wind* in three minutes.

I realise that a pop single should hit you where it hurts from the get-go. You listen to Chuck on 'Sweet Little Sixteen' or Kings of Leon on 'Revelry' and you get the damn picture. Both rock 'n swing hard; the singer has loads of charisma, the guitars cry and sing. But Hype Williams, Anthony Mandler, David Fincher, Sophie Muller – these video directors overburden the senses. It's as if I'd had three double espressos before I switched the TV on.

Let me tell you about the time I went to see *The Bourne Ultimatum* – I quickly understood why there's a billboard in LA that warns: 'Don't drive buzzed'. I'm being a bit one-dimensional here though.

Concentrating on a fast-paced, action-packed rollercoaster of a movie isn't actually that hard. Being able to keep pace with the storyline while salting popcorn, giving the Wii a spin and sending a text message – that could prove challenging. I feel like a twenty year old at a club when I'm watching Jason Bourne. I need something to do with my hands. Not a Jack Daniels in a shot glass to look cool but something to keep the element of my brain that's connected to my hands amused.

That's why they have perfected movies for home viewing. With Blu-ray I get suitable hi-def picture quality, five- or seven-channel sound and I don't have to be subjected to some imbecile exhorting: 'Watchit J, that oke's going to shoot you.'

I'm losing the plot here – not the movie's plot, but the overall plot. My brain just saunters off in its own alarming direction. I need something to do.

That damn Bourne movie has pressed my collective synapses into action. There's so much to focus on I feel as though I'm at a Stone Roses party in Manchester in the 1990s, except the strobe's going off a lot faster than I remember. I need to slow down.

Where's my copy of *In the Mood for Love*? No. That's too much high-colour saturation and perfect period piece ethic. I need something to chill my brain out. Ah, FTV.

I see all these sexy women on channel 184 and I wonder if Ava Gardner ever considered that her tumultuous relationship with The Voice would be edited down to a mere sound bite: 'There's only ten pounds of Frank, but there's a hundred and ten pounds of cock.'[2]

Ava was beautiful, glamorous and one helluva dame. Sure Gisele looks good and Bar Rafaeli, but I interpret them as Photoshopped gold diggers whereas Ava was stone-cold black and white brassy. And the legs on Barbara Stanwyck! Would I have to watch the whole of *Double Indemnity* just to see them?

I went to YouTube and found Dusty singing 'Son of a Preacher Man'. It's part of a new compilation I'm working on called *Dusty on Demand*. Wonderful clips collected on YouTube. The 'Dusty police' are trying to get the best ones off the site due to copyright issues but we anoraks know where to look.

How else would fans like us get to see clips of The King shaking hands on a movie set in the early 1960s? Elvis Presley Enterprises won't cough up the dough to buy the original footage. They're too busy selling 'Love me Tender' keychains made in China and 'Hound

Sorry, what were you saying?

Sandiso Ngubane

Is it possible for technology to cause one to lose one's sense of perspective and even lead to the underperformance of entire economies? According to Bryan Appleyard, a London *Sunday Times* columnist, distractions have that capacity. Appleyard quotes an American study which found that US$558 billion is lost to that country's economy every year thanks to technologies such as mobile phones, email, SMS and even social networks like Twitter and Facebook.[3]

Appleyard argues that we believe that checking emails while carrying out other tasks – something we define as multi-tasking – is a good thing ... but maybe it isn't.

The arrival of smart phones such as the Blackberry and iPhone has given rise to a new disorder known as Continuous Partial Attention (CPA), which results in a diminished attention span, leading to 'where was I' reactions and a struggle to refocus attention. Wordspy.com defines CPA as 'a state in which most of one's attention is on one primary task, but where one is also monitoring several background tasks in case something more interesting comes up'.[4]

Former Microsoft Vice-President and consultant Linda Stone, who coined the term CPA, argues that multi-tasking and CPA are two different attention strategies. Multi-tasking, she argues, is a beneficial strategy where each activity has a similar priority. Stone defines CPA as having a 'kind of vigilance that is not characteristic of multi-tasking. With CPA, we feel most alive when we're connected, plugged in and in the know'.[5]

The urge to answer that call, respond to emails, update your Facebook status or tweet in the middle of a social or business engagement are symptoms of this disorder.

CPA can also be dangerous. The *Daily Mail* reports that experts say driving under the influence of alcohol is actually less dangerous than using a hands-free phone. According to the UK's transport research laboratory, drivers engaged in a hands-free mobile conversation are 30% slower to react than those who are slightly over the alcohol limit.[6] It doesn't end there, though. Distractions are beginning to affect people in different ways, and they are not all related to technology.

Rugby player Bryan Habana reportedly

T R E N D   S N A C K

Sorry, what were you saying? *continued*

sent a cry for help to the Springboks' former visual performance and skills coach Dr Sheryl Calder.[7] Habana felt his performance was declining. The decline was attributed by Calder to the fact that he hadn't been on a visual skills programme for more than a year. The reason? Habana is a celebrity in demand; photo shoots and public engagements linked to endorsement deals had begun to interfere with his training programme. Calder says the visual performance programme should be prioritised by players since if visual skills are reduced, one loses judgement, and judgement errors are costly for professional sportsmen. Habana's story bespeaks a different type of distraction, but the end result is the same: a loss of focus is always detrimental to the task at hand or ultimate goal.

Technology and increasingly hectic lifestyles contribute to distraction, leading to underperformance and even possible fatality in some cases. The nature of our busy lives, filled with distraction, obstructs us from a peaceful life of contemplation, rational thought and measured decisions. 'Distractions from distraction by distraction' is modern man's predicament, says Maggie Jackson, the author of *Distraction: The Erosion of Attention and the Coming Dark Age.*[8]

Now, what was it that I was supposed to be doing?

T R E N D   S N A C K

Dog' bags for six year olds. The legacy (or at least part of it) resides on YouTube.

And how about that ugly chick – the one who can sing? Again, it sounds like Frankie – skinny runt with a voice from above. I should go back and check out the clip. Fat chick sings. It's a moment.

My life is like a James Ellroy novel. A whole lot happens but the report to my brain is made up of journalistic fragments. 'He woke up. The dogs barked snappy. Cold and dark outside until he opened his eyes. Then even more bleak as he recalled the night just past.' Talk about life imitating pop art.

At least I didn't end up in *Sin City* – greasy hair, razorblade smile, eaten by my own dog in the first scene. I'm beginning to miss the distinction between movies, reality TV and reality. Maybe I should be more like the guy on TV – I'd get recognised. Where's the remote so I can scan the hard-disk for some shows.

Nowadays everyone speaks in such clipped sentences. It's so difficult having conversations with my mother. My shorthand English seems rude and inappropriate but by the time she's finished her first scene I've sent five or six SMSs.

SMS is a revelation – far more significant than mobile or voice-over-IP. You can have major interactions about football and say unspeakable things about the ref when there are kids around.

I recently read such an incredible piece about the word 'like'. Rather than an unfortunate addition to the language that most English teachers would like to surgically remove from their students' frontal lobes, it does in fact act as a mini scene-opener. Because when one says 'like' you are about to act out a scene, an interpretation of an event.[9] Rather than simply telling the story you're about to act it out with all the body and facial gestures a music video performer might employ. 'So I was like (withering glance) forget about it (look of derision). You made the mistake (like duh) and you have to live with the consequences (Barack Obama nailing Hillary Clinton in the primaries).'

I was wondering if they'd find space for Dylan in the cellular content paradise. All this talk of thousands of songs on offer, but nothing to buy. I know the feeling – thousands of LPs but nothing to listen to. I sympathise with Imelda Marcos.

Now reducing Dylan to a sound bite or a single song or

performance – that would be a chore. Presley is so much easier. The whole of America voted for the image they'd most relish on a postage stamp. 'Young Elvis' won. 'Fat Vegas jumpsuit Elvis' lost. The entire fiasco had more to do with his estate's refusal to unlock his entire human existence in favour of a haloed, Technicolor, Royal Crown pomade 1950s-forever angel. But how about Dylan?

The thin, dusty Woody Guthrie folkie-like waif? The cool, electric poet laureate who stole Suze Rotolo's heart?[10] The amphetamine-charged rock 'n roll star who, while on tour in Manchester prefaced 'Like a Rolling Stone' with the instruction 'play fucking loud'. The born-again Jesus freak slowly losing his edge? The born-again old-timer with the withering, grating voice that won him Grammys? And they call Madonna the queen of reinvention!

The song that came to define a decade even in the face of The Beatles' chart assault gushed from his mind's pen: 'This long piece of vomit, 20 pages long, and out of it I took "Like a Rolling Stone" and made it as a single.'

For those of you too young to know (or too old to remember), a single was a seven-inch piece of black plastic that contained (in most cases) two songs (back to back). It was the most important carrier of recorded music before the LP (long player) hit the shelves and artists like The Beatles sold millions of them.

'Like a Rolling Stone' was so long (six minutes) it had to be split over the two sides of the Columbia seven-inch vinyl. DJs played the first side, then turned the damn thing around and spun the rest. The song is so significant that famed critic Greil Marcus wrote an entire book about it.[11] How would one reduce Dylan to a sound bite when four decades ago the single, the biggest music format, failed to condense his most vital outpouring? That's my problem with digital – it allows for unlimited amounts of content at your immediate disposal, yet you're driven to savour only the tiniest morsels.

Dylan has had the last laugh. He will always have the last laugh. On receiving his Grammy Lifetime Achievement Award in 1991 he memorably delivered 'Masters of War' (from 1963's *The Freewheelin' Bob Dylan*) as the first Gulf War commenced. It was a brief statement about the relevance of popular music in the broader world – today replaced with red-carpet interviews and wardrobe malfunctions as opposed to sincere, meaningful performances on 'music's most [un] important night'.

So far there have been eight instalments of the Dylan 'bootleg series' featuring previously unreleased material. Most of it is far better than unfortunate episodes such as *Dylan and the Dead* (the worst Dylan album and the worst Grateful Dead album).

A sharp-witted hack once quipped that if enough multi-CD compendiums were released by Sinatra, Presley and The Beatles, he might have to defer his kid's college education. It would take a few years just to listen to all of Dylan's notable stuff. And by June 2009 I may have been crushed by the massive weight of the *Neil Young Archives Volume 1: 1963–1972*. One hundred and sixteen tracks, four DVDs and four CDs. I used to spend weekends getting through episodes of *The Sopranos*, *The Simpsons* and *Will & Grace*. Neil will ensure that I miss any prospect of future personal TV exposure.

Recorded music and film is able to capture what may have been lost in notation in centuries past. For example, great classical pianists are still presenting their interpretations of works by Bach, Beethoven and Mozart. But the composer may have had to forego small yet valuable details when putting pen to stave. Would Shakespeare have been totally happy with Olivier's performance as Hamlet? Modern recording technology in music and movies means we're left with indelible images and, with the growth of technology, an ever-expanding cauldron of experiences. I know I can't keep up.

The net's widening and I'm sinking fast. Nothing will ever bruise my consciousness again even though I have access to enough digital content to go on searching forever.

I suppose I should be happy though. I'm able to gulp from an overflowing chalice of recorded content. The last fifteen years especially have been a high point for American television comedy and drama – production values and scripts have often been better than those produced by Hollywood.

And how about the Internet?

I began collecting music at the dawn of the ether age – I couldn't have tracked down a mono original of The Beatles' *Revolver* had it not been for GEMM[12] and 'ePay'. As a fan, it's a distinct pleasure having access to books, movies and music on demand (with maybe a two-week wait for postage).

As bandwidth expands, high-quality downloads will surpass physical products such as DVDs and CDs for the most part. Aficionados will still track down 1A LP stampers and first-edition books while most people will be more than happy with an on-demand *Desperate Housewives* marathon. Personally, I'm not sure as to whether or not I should embrace the wave of tiny technological revolutions or enforce a Luddite mentality.

While I'm not about to join the African division of the Flat Earth Movement, I do feel that this excess of information and material simply aims to fill up our time like so many extramural activities for teenagers (remember when we rode our bikes in the street). I guess at any time, in societies everywhere, power and money were able to buy stuff to fill up time. Now more people have money and things cost less so there you go.

As for all the instant revisionism that exists with DVDs, it's another subject that's getting out of control. These 'director's cuts' are almost as prevalent as UN spats between Israel and Iran. You stare at the shelves like a novice trying to figure out which version of *Blade Runner* or *The Godfather* to purchase. You need to trawl the chatrooms for advice before you click on Amazon. And with Blu-ray I'll have a third copy of *Jailhouse Rock*.

Is there a definitive version of the first *American Pie* or did I miss something when Shannon Elizabeth took off her clothes? Are there deleted scenes from *Superbad* on some yet-to-be-discovered forum? And once the artist/director is no longer with us that means their ability to edit their catalogue reverts to the 'rights owner' – a simple opportunity for commercial exploitation at every turn.

I'm back to making that music video. Great writers (songwriters that is) and one helluva singer and performer. All right, I've made a slight revision to my earlier plan. I need a singer and a performer – in a single package. They should sing 'live' in my video. Then in a couple of years time we'll have a digital download accompanied by a physical Blu-ray disc with selected out-takes, which can be updated via the web. And if there are a few bum notes, no problem – in 30 years the 'rights owner' will get the offspring of the musicians to re-record the backing tracks. I'll get a good engineer to put everything down on ProTools – we could have multiple takes for the 'special deluxe edition' for release once the artist fades from view or tragically dies at the tender age of 27. You couldn't make this stuff up!

Notes and references

1 Since Michael Jackson's death on 25 June 2009 the numbers have skyrocketed.
2 Anthony Summers and Robbyn Swan, *Sinatra: The Life* (Corgi, 2006).
3 Bryan Appleyard, *Sunday Times* (London), 20 July 2008.

4   'Continuous Partial Attention (CPA)', Wordspy.com, www.wordspy.com/words/
    continuouspartialattention.asp (accessed 29 June 2009)

5   Linda Stone, 'Fine Dining with Mobile Devices'. Huffington Post Online,
    www.huffingtonpost.com/linda-stone/fine-dining-with-mobile-d_b_80819.
    html (accessed 29 June 2009).

6   Fiona Macrae, 'Hands Free Phones Slated as Riskier than Drinking and Driving'.
    Daily Mail, 1 March 2009.

7   Peter Bills, 'Habana Sends Out an SOS'. *The Sunday Independent*, 15 March 2009.

8   Maggie Jackson, *Distraction: The Erosion of Attention and the Coming Dark Age*
    (Prometheus Books, 2008).

9   Thomas de Zengotita, *Mediated: How the Media Shapes your World and the Way
    you Live in it* (Bloomsbury, 2005).

10 Suze Rotolo is an American artist who dated Bob Dylan on and off in the 1960s.
    She is best known to his fans as the woman with him on the cover of his album
    The Freewheelin' Bob Dylan. This is according to the Internet Movie Database at
    www.imdb.com (accessed 29 June 2009).

11 Greil Marcus, *Like a Rolling Stone: Bob Dylan at the Crossroads* (Faber and Faber,
    2005).

12 GEMM is an online music marketplace at www.gemm.com (accessed 29 June
    2009).

Raymond Kurzweil, *The Singularity is Near* (Penguin Books, 2006).
David Thomson, *The Whole Equation: A History of Hollywood* (Abacus, 2004).

FLUX OBSERVATION

The unplugged revolution

Loren Phillips

THE INSISTENT cry of an alarm clock pierces your sleep. Another day has arrived. You drag your body out of bed. Your first thought is of coffee – the only thing that offers a bit of solace. You switch on the kettle. The toaster spits out some processed bread. You read the packaging. *More* packaging. You wonder why they needed to add extra vitamins. Sigh. They must've stripped them all out in the first place and then replaced them with a laboratory-manufactured version. You dress, brush your teeth and make your way to the car. On a good day it takes half an hour to drive in to the office. You listen to a language-learning CD or Mozart, trying to compensate for the mindless waste of time that is rush-hour traffic. Finally, you get to the office. You switch on your computer to a flood of emails. Your cellphone starts buzzing with birthday reminders and text messages. Fax machines and printers spit out paper. Clutter.

In the past twenty years, these devices have infiltrated our daily lives. And despite the many benefits they offer – communication, travel, entertainment – these machines and the technologies that underpin them also have the equal and opposite effect of being too consuming, of weighing us down. Everything is 'on' and more and more people are consciously opting to switch off.

We are witnessing the beginning of an 'unplugged' revolution that has people going back to nature, exploring spirituality and embracing traditional practices such as crafts and gardening.

The pitfalls of the digital landscape

People are beginning to question some aspects of digital life, such as being 'always on' and permanently available, seeing it increasingly as a downfall of 21st-century life. Our brains are largely being rewired to skim information. Reading is becoming less of a leisure activity. Web journalists have to use a prescriptive method in their writing, including external links and bullet points to make content easier for their readers to consume. People generally display shorter attention spans, amplified by a wave of messages that they are bombarded with every day. The quantity of messages has long superseded the quality.

George Hegel, the 18th-century German philosopher, proposed the 'Pendulum Theory',[1] stating that once a certain phase in history has reached its necessary conclusion, it will be replaced by its equal and opposite phase. A resolution is then reached, which replaces the previous models. With this in mind, it is easy to see how living amidst all the gadgetry and technological clutter, there would be a pull in the opposite direction towards living a more simple, clutter-free life with more time available for the things that matter most – family and friends.

Hopefully we will eventually establish some kind of balance, whereby the technologies that we live with happily co-exist with a more natural way of life that humans innately yearn for. People are remembering the magic that lies in 'being' as opposed to always 'doing'.

Who's the boss?

Mobile phones and the Internet have their place. They have helped us progress in a completely new and necessary direction. Take Internet publishing, for example – it has single-handedly helped spare entire forests from being chopped down and pulped. That means more oxygen for us and better management of the huge ecological calamity that faces our planet. At the same time, Internet publishing has given everybody with access a voice. People publish blogs and even their own writing or photo journal with the help of sites like Lulu.com.

These technologies are a reality and an unavoidable eventuality, but it seems that in many cases, they have overstepped their boundaries and taken over our lives; instead of helping us, they own us. They own our time, they own our relationships, and research shows that they could even be harming us.

Healthy boundaries

We are entering relatively unchartered territory when it comes to wireless technology and the full long-term effects are not necessarily known. A growing body of research shows that mobile and wireless technology can have a detrimental effect on our health. These studies indicate that government regulations on the public health issues related to the use of technology are outdated and legislation is in serious need of revision. Studies are being published online to help publicise the growing need to re-align governmental regulations regarding wireless technology. Several blogs and sites have been set up to publicise and discuss these findings, such as The EMR (Electromagnetic Radiation) Network, a non-profit organisation with a website that is updated with new findings almost monthly. The EMR Safety blog was also created in 2008. It links to numerous other sites and hosts video talks by experts on the subject of EMR.

On 25 June 2009 a comprehensive study was published that investigates the link between mobile phones and brain tumours. The author, who has appeared on *Larry King Live* and published several articles on the subject, Dr Vini G. Khurana, set up the 'Mobile Phone Base Station Public Health Advisory Webpage' with the aim of raising public awareness about our global immersion in low-intensity EMR. This form of radiation emanates from sources such as power lines, radio, TV antennae and WiFi systems. Khurana states conclusively in his extensive report that 'mobile phone usage for ten or more years approximately doubles a user's chance of being diagnosed with a brain tumour ... on the same side of the head as that preferred for mobile telephony'.[2]

It is clear that we are seeing only the tip of the iceberg in terms of the long-term effects of wireless technologies on our health, and committed groups are working towards publicising the dangers with which we are increasingly being confronted.

Mezzanine-level communication

The popular gadget review site Gizmodo recently ran a poll for its users, questioning whether their gadgets make them happy or sad. One user made the following comment: 'I admit that I'm addicted to gadgets but I also voted *sad* in the above poll. I like to think that *technological minimalism* will eventually come into vogue and advanced technology will be integrated into our lives without demanding so much of our attention.'[3]

For all the connections and community-building that the Internet allows, it seems that it is not bringing us much happiness. Often we pawn off our interactions to this 'mezzanine-level communication', such as cancelling a date with a quick SMS or breaking up with a lover in an email, not accepting responsibility for, or ownership of, our response.

This has the converse effect of driving people apart, instead of bringing them together, which should be the aim of such communication tools.

These devices are also affecting family life. They keep us from being 'emotionally present' for the people who are most important to us. Non-attentiveness is starting to affect personal relationships throughout the wired (and wireless) world. The devices that are meant to facilitate communication are actually taking something away from the exchanges that matter most. Somewhere along the line, we have forgotten how to prioritise our communication.

Carol Affleck, a research psychologist from the youth market consulting company Youth Focus, agrees:

> I have had many instances in focus group feedback where parents tell us they struggle to communicate with their teenagers at the dinner table as their teens are chatting on MXit. Similarly teens themselves tell us that they get frustrated when trying to chat face-to-face to a friend who is simultaneously chatting on MXit and interacting with them via grunts, monosyllables and hmmms, etc. On the other hand, research has reported that when asked what kind of leisure time contact they favour, the vast majority said they prefer to hang out with friends in the real world than interact in the online world. That appears to be the next best thing when the real person is not available. All in all it is clear that teens love to be in contact 24/7, and that not being in the loop is like death to them.[4]

Living with less

The global financial crisis, which has resulted in recession in many countries, has slowed the pace of these economies. Always eager to find a silver lining, I understand this recession to be a necessary and possibly even a good thing for the future of global citizens and the planet. Consumers are being forced into a position where they consider their current way of life with greater care and question unnecessary purchases.

The recession has forced simplicity on many, and people who had lived comfortably through the boom times are now finding the joy in living with less. It means they get to spend more quality time with their families as leisure time increasingly moves into the home as the hub of entertainment. We are even seeing a new trend in the USA that harks back to the turn of the previous century. According to *The New York Times* there has been an increase in the sale of old-fashioned canning products, and AllRecipes.com reports a 109% increase in page views to articles covering canning, jams, pickling and preserves.[5] This type of practice is done at home, with the family, and resonates with a 'humanness' with which many have lost touch. Home gardening and handicraft are also coming back into vogue, echoing trends witnessed during the Great Depression.

The Slow Movement as a lifestyle choice is spreading around the globe. Realising that the current pace of life does not foster enjoyment but breeds discontent, people are consciously slowing down and taking time to enjoy the things that make life worth living. 'Slow Food',[6] founded by Carlo Petrini in Italy, is an organisation that encourages ethical consumption and seeks to promote regional produce with an emphasis on family-owned farms. Although the Slow Movement is not new, it is interesting to note how it is slowly transmuting into other areas of consumer life, such as fashion and design.

'Slow Fashion' aims to replace the previous and outdated 'fast-fashion' model. Here, traceability and ethical manufacturing are becoming key areas of discernment for the consumer. The pace is slower, which promotes well-thought-out designs and does not encourage obsolescence after only a couple of seasons. Every link in the value chain stands to benefit, from the person who procures the yarn to the machinist who sews the garment, to the retailer who can market these stories to the public.

This idea stands firmly in contrast to the pace of life that we have become accustomed to. The slowing pace is indicative of a broader trend moving towards 'Slow Design', which seeks to emphasise and celebrate the actual creative process behind design, and move away from the treadmill of fast design that spews out products that are not well considered and are ultimately wasteful, such as products that are manufactured without using recyclable-grade plastics.

In her presentation at Design Indaba 2009, in Cape Town, trend expert Li Edelkoort discussed a mood that she termed 'unplugged'. This idea revolves around young people opting for and exploring rural settings. It's a movement from the urban to the pastoral where the focus is on all things acoustic, as opposed to electric; it celebrates the spoken word over digital communication, which signifies a yearning for more personal forms of communication. In fact, we are seeing this trend play itself out in various ways. A new iPhone application allows people to send postcards to their friends around the world straight from their devices,[7] which echoes an application on Facebook called Peggymail,[8] launched in 2008, which also sends physical postcards to real addresses, helping families stay connected no matter what their online status may be.

Reconnecting

People are realising or simply remembering the power of connecting to the natural world as a source of inspiration and creativity. The 'unplugged' revolution promotes connecting with the moment, something Buddhists have been advocating for centuries, as the way to find one's own truth and happiness.

Mindfulness is described as having the ability to expand each moment, allowing more space to be filled with creativity, joy and peace – which people are increasingly recognising as being more important than driving the latest model car.

The speed of invention and the uptake has allowed technology to dictate the pace of our lives. Now it is up to us to take the lead and reassign technology its correct place and function: to enable us. Technology is an important aspect of business and social life but it needs to be kept in its place. It is necessary to re-establish a workable balance between digital and natural life that fosters personal growth and promotes interpersonal relationships.

Notes

1 'What is the Hegelian Theory of History?' eNotes.com, 2009, www.enotes.com/history-fact-finder/philosophy/what-hegelian-theory-history (accessed 14 July 2009).

2 Vini Khurana, 'Mobile Phone Base Station Public Health Advisory', 25 June 2009, www.brain-surgery.us/mast.html (accessed 22 July 2009). Other sources for this information include www.emrnetwork.org/news.htm and www.emr-safety. blogspot.com (accessed 20 July 2009).

3 See www.gizmodo.com (accessed 20 July 2009).

4 See www.youthfocus.co.za (accessed 8 September 2009).

5 See www.allrecipes.com (accessed 20 July 2009).

6 'Slow Food'. Wikipedia.org, 2009, www.en.wikipedia.org/wiki/Slow_food (accessed 20 July 2009).

7   Susanna Haynie, 'iPhone App Creates and Sends Real Postcards'. Springwise.com,
    14 July 2009, www.springwise.com/life_hacks/gopostal/ (accessed 20 July 2009).
8   Jenny Lau, 'Snail Mail App for Facebook Users'. Springwise.com, 10 November
    2009, www.springwise.com/life_hacks/snail_mail_application_for_fac/
    (accessed 20 July 2009).

From silence to violence

How do you define sexual identity in the 21st century?

Dr Marlene Wasserman

Dr Marlene Wasserman is a Clinician in Private Practice, a sexual medicine consultant, a couple and sex therapist and an activist for sexual and reproductive health and rights. She began her career with a BA Honours in Social Work from the University of the Witwatersrand, after which her interest turned to family therapy and she gained a Master of Social Science degree in Clinical Social Work, cum laude, from the University of the Orange Free State. She has been awarded certificates from institutions in Canada and the USA, among them a Doctorate in Human Sexuality, and accreditation as a Couple and Sex Therapist from the AASECT (American Association of Sex Educators, Counsellors and Therapists), the most highly recognised accrediting society in the world.

During family therapy sessions her attention frequently focused on the inter-action between parents, instilling in her a passion for understanding intimate relationships and sexuality. Today she continues to pursue further training in sexual medicine and couple and sex therapy.

Wasserman passionately shares her knowledge by lecturing part-time at the University of Cape Town's Medical School, presenting papers at scientific meet-ings and forums around the world, and by using radio, TV and writing as edu-cational platforms. Her books include *Dr Eve's Sex Book: A Guide for Young Adults, Pillowbook,* and *Ageing and Sexuality,* and she also devotes time to her website, www.dreve.co.za.

AM a clinical sexologist and a couples and sex therapist. Recently, as I sat in my armchair deeply absorbed in a new client's story, I withdrew for a moment and for the first time it dawned on me, with amazement, how incredibly absurd this situation would appear to someone witnessing this process from the outside.

Imagine a stranger sitting on your couch; within moments you are privy to the story of his lack of semen, his penis which seems to have shrunk; or her vagina that will not open or her orgasms that can only happen when she is lashing a client.

The majority of the courageous, curious and often deeply troubled clients who seek out my professional skills have probably never told these things to anyone else. And perhaps you too have never discussed or disclosed to anyone the private, intimate and sexual world you inhabit.

Allow me to re-identify myself. I am a highly privileged person who has earned the right, due to extensive professional training, to learn about human behaviour, specifically sexual and relationship behaviour, and as I lock my office door every day I am more confused than the day before.

For example, one day I am convinced that the majority of women can't have consensual sex with strangers for fun, that they reinforce the societal construct which states that women need to be in a 'loving relationship' with a partner in order to want and enjoy sex.[1] The following day I will be running a workshop for young adult women and abandon this theory as the women tell me that the best sex they have is with random people in clubs, and that kissing girls is cool in spite of them being straight.

Sexuality does not occur in a vacuum, but rather exists within the context of unique individualistic experiences affected by larger social issues, such as politics, economics and religion.

As I share my observations about, and predictions for, 2010, bear in mind that I have already recused myself by claiming confusion when working in my world of sexuality and relationships – according to the practices and principles of healthy sexuality, sexual and reproductive health and relationships, this world is fluid and ever-changing, and nothing is 'normal'.

Monks, medicine and the law

In the beginning there was man and there was woman. Man left home and hunted for food while woman gathered seeds, including extra semen from men at the campsite just in case her man's seed did not arrive on time to ensure the continuation of the species. She was considered a goddess, a magical creature who birthed children. She also gave a man who found her attractive, an erection, quite spontaneously, just by standing near him or having him think about her.

But as communities grew, their need to move to larger spaces brought new jobs and roles for both men and women. The plough changed sexuality as it was known. Oxen or horses were used to pull ploughs, and men, being in less demand, found themselves out of work. Women remained in charge of seed-gathering and taking care of children. Men helped the women gather, trading and exchanging with others, thereby planting the first seeds of commerce, but felt disempowered in their own homes. They began to explore new parts of the world, which often meant stealing both the property and people, or women, of other men in order to accumulate wealth, status and power. Rape and pillage began in this way, forever changing the status and power relationships between men and women.

By now religion was the voice of authority in communities and it began to dictate the ways in which sexual relationships were conducted. Somehow this trend remained unchanged through the centuries, becoming more profound and entrenched by the time of the 21st century. Religion dictated the sexual mores that are still in existence today. Some of these beliefs are: no pre-marital sex ('Does oral sex mean sex?' teens wonder); no extra-marital sex (which, until three years ago in South Africa, excluded same-sex couples); sex in the missionary position to increase the chances of reproduction ('I want my clitoris stimulated, not my vagina greased for hours!' scream women under men made ignorant in part by religious teachings); and, sex with one lifelong partner only.

As medicinal and scientific discoveries were made, a strong, scientific voice that emphasised the importance of provable truths emerged and, by the end of the 19th century, this voice was in serious competition with religion for control over people's sexuality. It also influenced morality, determining what was 'normal' and what was 'pathological'.

Is there any scientific research on how 'frequently' one should masturbate? Yet, an illness called 'masturbatory insanity' was a respected psychiatric illness commonly diagnosed in men (of course, not in women, as it was not considered that they masturbated).

Once people gather in groups, laws are needed to control their behaviour. So it came to be that legal structures were established that controlled and regulated people's sexuality. Of course, we need the law to protect us from harmful sexual behaviour such as non-consensual, violent sexual invasions of people's bodies (including adults and children). This is not a trend. It is the basic right of every citizen to sexual protection under the law.

These developments combined to make previously unacceptable sexual expressions, such as homosexuality, acceptable. Until 1986, medicine classified homosexuality as a psychiatric illness in the diagnostic 'bible', the *Diagnostic and Statistic Manual* (DSM); religion condemned homosexuals outright as sinners; and, 'sodomy' was an illegal act punishable by the law.

In the 1960s, the scientific medical work of Masters and Johnson gave rise to the discipline of Sex Therapy. A new profession emerged to control and regulate our sexuality and relationships, and to pathologise them further by seeking to define 'normal' sexuality.

In the decades prior to 2010, extremely important social movements and events occurred that have had a more significant impact on our sexuality than the narrow medical model, contributing to redefining what is considered 'normal'. In the 1960s, there was the gay liberation movement and the availability of oral contraception that offered women sexual and reproductive freedom; in the 1970s, feminism arose, and there were more women in the workplace; in the 1980s, HIV/AIDS; in the 1990s, democracy in South Africa and the development and spread of a culture of violence.

Let's examine current trends unfolding against the background of this short history.

Unfolding trends

Childhood sexuality
With South Africa claiming the highest incidence of child abuse and

an increase in the abuse of children by other children and children selling their siblings for sex, we cannot afford to be silent about childhood sexuality.

Comprehensive sexuality education has to be introduced as early as pre-school, and parents need support and education. A fear-based approach must be eliminated in favour of a positive approach that champions responsible sexual behaviour. The first rule when dealing with young children is to recognise that when children are masturbating they are soothing themselves into bliss. They are not having kinky sexual thoughts as they have not yet developed any. Silence and punitive responses will contribute towards them not reaching the necessary sexual milestones that will ensure they become healthy sexual adults.

In March 2008, with no fanfare, possibly the most important vaccination was launched. It is a vaccination that prevents Human Papillomavirus (HPV). HPV is a sexually transmitted infection that causes genital warts and cervical cancer (a lethal cancer, since it advances rapidly before producing symptoms). It is the most common form of cancer affecting women in South Africa.[2] Getting your child vaccinated will prevent her from contracting HPV.[3] Now that's something worth making a trend.

Teenage sexuality

Teens are the group at highest risk in South Africa and sub-Saharan Africa for HIV/AIDS, Sexually Transmitted Infections (STIs) and pregnancy. There has been an acceptance that the cornerstone of government health policy – Abstinence, Be Faithful, Condomise (ABC) – has not been effective and that instead, 'responsible' sexuality should be taught to teens. This entails offering as much factual information as is needed as well as teaching skills to negotiate situations and think about one's own role in certain sexual situations – both the consequences and rewards that result from decisions made.

Teens are having a lot of sexual play – real and virtual. Due to absent parents, parents who withhold vital information on sexuality from their children, or who prevent their access to information or services, teens are at tremendous risk.

Sexual content distributed on mobile phones and online continues to seduce, confuse, abuse and excite teens. It's called the triple-A effect: Anonymous, Affordable and Accessible. Watching YouTube videos about the speculated death by erotic asphyxiation of *Kill Bill* star David Carridine; seeing videos of their friends making out with other friends; or seeing a photo of their girlfriend showing off her genitals; these are becoming standard entertainment for teens.

Toying with one's sexuality – boys using make-up, or girls butching themselves up or switching sexual orientation for the night – can be fun. But when no conversations with adults or sexual education are available, this can result in curious, confused and sometimes depressed (even suicidal) teenagers with ill-defined sexual identities. As activists and non-governmental organisations lobby against violence and homophobia, young people will feel freed up to come out and will need support.

Ageing sexuality

By 2020, 9% of the world's population will be over 65 years old. Researching and writing my book *Ageing and Sexuality: A 21st Century Guide to Lifelong Sensuality*[4] increased my awareness of how strong and subtle ageism is, and how this will be challenged through the actions of ageing people. Living long, and living long in a healthy and vital manner, will become the normative expectation of all of us.

Medicine is helping to dignify ageing by focusing on the importance of lifestyle factors as a way of preventing chronic diseases and, of course, on providing effective treatments. All this allows people to continue to be sexual as they age.

Marketing plastic surgery, hormone replacement therapy for men and women, HIV/AIDS education, dating opportunities and computer lessons for 'graying surfers' will be some of the strongest new trends. Hence the birth of sexual medicine as a new field in medicine. Sexual medicine manages the sexual dysfunctions that result from chronic diseases which are almost always as a result of poor, even dangerous lifestyle choices people make over the years. It also speaks to the newest and most important focus of ageing: hormone replacement for men and women.

Relationships

Increased mobility, technological developments, pressure to perform financially, the need to acquire status, ageing well and changes in the way that we understand the concept of 'love' all leave the relationships of today almost unrecognisable from what they were a few years ago.

Living Apart Together (LAT) will become more common as two people in a committed form of relationship, choose to live in different cities or countries, houses or even beds. Ageing people tell me how they delight in their freedom once their kids have left home, followed by a divorce or the death of a spouse. Starting a new relationship may include nights of blissful sex but days in one's own home, and separate holidays with one's own kids.

Fidelity and the definition thereof, is being significantly challenged. Does it mean no chatting with strangers online? Never looking at a pornographic image? No meaningless sexual play with a paid sex worker or happy endings with a massage therapist? Faithfulness remains a core need for people of all ages and stages of life – but maintaining it in a world filled with sexual opportunity is challenging.

Add in the risk factors of increased recreational drug use, alcohol and stress, as well as the trend to stay and make it work. Consider that infidelity is no longer a legal reason for divorce. Just to confuse us even more, another very prevalent trend is the acceptance that a relationship has a sell-by date, a limited lifespan. So when it no longer adds value or feels good, get out ethically and elegantly. People are left to battle it out in very trying situations on their own.

Cheating is so common one has to normalise it and treat it as part of the relationship cycle, especially those that last for many years. For example, the normative cycle of a relationship is: marry, have an affair, work it out, have another affair, divorce and move on to next marriage – or a variation thereof. The hurt, betrayal and unbearable shattering of hearts that cheating brings makes it very untrendy behaviour. Thus the media should portray situations of how to avoid cheating; and should stop sensationalising and glamorising celebrity affairs. Rather teach people how to keep relationships vital and tight with 'NO ENTRY' signs at every entrance.

Love needs redefining. People are learning to shift expectations. No longer does the joined-at-the-hip relationship work. For love to work in the future we have to grow individuals into self-sufficient, independent, happy people who share and care for each other but never compromise their value systems to have relationships.

Unfortunately, a form of 'love' in this country is gender-based violence and femicide. It sounds crazy to call it love, I know. But then again, when a behaviour pattern is so common, one has to see it as a trend. I can have a full day of woman after woman on the couch describing a 'loving' husband. This is the man who tells her what to wear, how to do her hair, locks her out of the house at night when she comes home a little later than promised, and withholds love and affection when she is not in the mood for sex – because he regularly pushes her around. She tells me she loves him so much – yet cannot understand why she cannot have sexual play with him.

Gender inequality, poverty and a lack of negotiating power lead to violence becoming a form, albeit a terrible one, of loving.

Thanks to recent legislation, same-sex unions are by now passé in many communities. The challenge is to take out the heterosexual-normative role expectations and allow same-sex couples to formulate their own rules and construct their own roles. Who cares who wears the pants?

I am beginning to see interesting creative sexualities developing out of same-sex marriages. For example, among two men the trend seems to be to incorporate a third partner as an optional way of being sexually faithful. Once again, honesty seems to be at the core of a successful relationship.

Sexual behaviour

Men having sex with men, and women having sex with women is a recognisable trend. Much more attention needs to be given to this so as to prevent HIV/AIDS and STIs in this high-risk group – education, more media conversations and mainstreaming this sexuality may help to keep it responsible and rewarding.

In 2012 the updated DSM V manual will be launched. Sexual trends have been noted giving rise to changes in the medical status of certain conditions. For example, 'gender identity disorder' will no longer be present in its current form. It has been noted that it is not a sexual dysfunction. This is a huge leap for transsexual people who can be treated with dignity and thus have a greater chance of making a successful transition. One hopes this change will encourage transsexuals to come out earlier and thus gain access to treatment, preventing distress and confusion.

The other significant change in the DSM V would be the elimination of Bondage, Discipline, Sado-Masochism (BDSM) as a disorder, an issue still up for debate and discussion. If you are a person who consensually likes to be restrained, paddled, whipped, humiliated and treated by a master as his or her slave, are you mentally ill? Are you a Paraphiliac BDSM (where behaviour is recurrent) or just a person who likes to play with it to heighten an otherwise vanilla sexual lifestyle? The trend towards glamorising BDSM is highly visible in mainstream media, clothing and advertisements. It gets confusing when your partner or healthcare professional calls you 'kinky' while you are just imitating Madonna.

Sex toys are über trendy – something I anticipate will grow and grow. One reason is that sex toys have finally entered the hallowed halls of medicine via sexual medicine. And doctors, blushing and somewhat awkward, are sending patients with dry vaginas, or loss of vaginal sensation due to menopause or medication, to shop for sex toys. Many doctors keep stock of water- or silicone-based lubricant to sell to patients for these conditions.

Sexual pharmaceuticals

Ten years ago Viagra arrived in our world. And suddenly every Tom, Dick and Harry disclosed that they suffer from erectile dysfunction. Today clinicians routinely need to ask every patient about their erectile status as it is a marker of possible cardiovascular disease.

Currently there are three drugs, phosphodiesterase type 5 inhibitors (PDE5I), used to treat erectile dysfunction safely and effectively,

Something queer about sexual identity

Milisuthando Bongela

Before the turn of the century, queer people and queer culture were pretty much invisible. Aided by the media, the law, politics and religious doctrine served to keep the boundaries between public and private spaces solid and impermeable. Sex was easier done than said, was only natural and right between a man and a woman, and deviants to this hegemonic discourse on sexuality were banished to their closets.

Over the past few years, the notion of 'queerness', as a derisive alternative to heterosexuality has been challenged by 20- and 30-something year olds who have matured as adults in a South Africa that has undergone a paradigm shift in perceptions of what is moral and immoral. The mere fact that the word 'queer', originally a derogatory term used to describe homosexuals, bisexuals and transsexuals, is used so candidly in popular culture is indicative of the way in which queer people have taken ownership of how society views them.

Today, freedom of sexual orientation is a badge of honour that a growing number of urban youth across all races wear proudly for many different reasons. It's not surprising to meet people who tell you what they do for a living, how many pets they have and their sexual orientation, all within the first hour.

Facebook is exemplary of this cut-to-the-chase approach or 'selfvertising', as one of the first fields you fill in when signing up asks whether you are looking for men, women or both.

In 2010, the demographic of same-sex couples vastly differs from that of ten years ago, as a growing number of heterosexual women are getting involved in relationships with each other or lesbian and bisexual women. Some do it 'just to try it', as in the lyrics of pop star Katy Perry's hit song 'I Kissed a Girl', while others, particularly an increasing number of 20-, 30- and 40-something year old urban black women, engage in long-term relationships with women because they are indefinitely 'tired' of dating men.

Culture-hopping is another significant trend where people immerse themselves in queer culture when they are not queer, the same way some people adopt and practise Jewish culture when they are not Jewish. The popular annual Mother City Queer Project party is always attended by some of these

T R E N D   S N A C K

Something queer about sexual identity *continued*

culture-hoppers, many of whom are not homosexual or even bisexual.

Media such as TV brought queer culture into our living rooms and consciousness, with gay or lesbian people being portrayed, not necessarily accurately, but as likeable to those who were homophobic or clueless about queer people. But even more than television, the Internet has played the biggest role in shaping how we communicate, what we have access to and who and what we associate with.

The Internet embodies the notion of choice, which is what sexuality in the 21st century is about. Yes there are people who are naturally going to identify with one type of sexual orientation, be it homosexual or heterosexual – but the really interesting trend is the increasing number of people who are openly oscillating between these various types of sexual identity.

What's happening now and what will continue to happen is a reactionary deflation of the notion that heterosexuality is the only cornerstone of a moral society. Its 'rightness' and 'normality' is being challenged as more and more people, through interaction with cultures and lifestyles they previously would have feared and felt prejudiced about, are experiencing the non-perilous effects of 'colouring outside the lines' and deconstructing their social conditioning on the subject of gender and sexuality.

T R E N D   S N A C K

namely, Viagra, Levitra and Cialis. A trend to avoid is the temptation to buy cheap imitations of these scheduled drugs. It could kill you. Another three PDE5Is are awaiting approval from the Medicines Control Council so there will be an increased sense of safety – and probably an increased misuse of these drugs.

But the biggest sexual revolution of all awaits us yet – female sexual desire disorder affects 43% of pre-menopausal women in the world. At present there is no medication available to treat this disabling dysfunction. Pharmaceutical company Boehringer Ingelheim is currently developing a drug, Flibanserin, to be launched on the market for women who meet the diagnostic criteria for this disorder. Buy shares in the company now if you are a serious trendoid.

A trend I am hoping will grow is the safe and informed use of hormone replacement for women as well as for men. Pharmaceutical manufacturers, gynaecologists and sexual medicine consultants are deeply committed to overcoming myths and fears and providing scientific information to consumers about the importance, safety and efficacy of hormone replacement once a woman has undergone a comprehensive history-taking and standard medical work-ups.

HIV/AIDS

As a responsible clinician and sexual educator it is with a heavy heart that I add HIV/AIDS to my list of trends. The trend to practise unsafe risky sex continues as indicated by our ever-increasing numbers of infected people.[5] And the trend to be blasé about condoms but not increase our correct or consistent use of them leaves me feeling somewhat despondent.

How can we make condom use sexy? How can we get people to have only one sexual partner at a time? How can we make circumcision a trend that all men will want to follow because it is cool to be cut? We know from robust research that these are protective and preventive measures that cut down on transmission.

I want the act of going for Voluntary Counselling and Testing (VCT) to be a regular and responsible activity that every sexually active person does. I want access to Antiretrovirals (ARV) to be a right, for people to know that taking them is not just a passing phase until they feel better now that the government has been beaten into taking responsibility by the Treatment Action Campaign (TAC) and is providing them for free. 'Live positively on ARVs' should become a mantra.

*   *   *

My trend wish-list for 2010 includes: taking the silence out of sexuality; believing you are being the trendiest mom on the block by taking your child for a HPV vaccination and getting your man or your son circumcised. If we give people sexual language and a voice, the violence may lessen, the negotiation and disclosures increase. I wish for the recognition of the importance of sexual health and functioning at any age. Being respectful in your lifestyle and avoiding chronic diseases for as long as possible will enable you to get hard or juicy without swallowing a prescribed drug. And, as you age, I hope that, without hesitation, you will swallow the pills, invest in hormone replacements, vibrators, cock rings and most of all, loving, respectful and caring relationships. Now that's really hot.

Notes

1   Reference can be made here to the Basson model. Rosemary Basson is the director of the Program in Sexual Medicine at the University of British Columbia. She constructed a new model of female sexual response incorporating the importance of emotional intimacy, sexual stimuli and relationship satisfaction. Basson's model acknowledges that female sexual functioning is more complex and circuitous than male sexual functioning and that it is dramatically and significantly affected by numerous psychosocial issues, including satisfaction with the relationship, self-image and previous negative sexual experiences. For more information, see Association of Reproductive Health Professionals, www.arhp.org/Publications-and-Resources/Clinical-Fact-Sheets/Female-Sexual-Response (accessed 1 July 2009).

2 This is according to research conducted by the South African Medical Research Council's Gender and Health Research Unit. See www.mrc.ac.za/gender/reports.htm (accessed 1 July 2009).

3 According to the Centre for Disease Control and Prevention, the vaccine is given in three shots over a six-month period. It is routinely recommended for eleven- and twelve-year-old girls and also for girls and women aged thirteen to twenty-six who have not yet been vaccinated or completed the vaccine series.

4 The book is published by Oshun, 2009.

5 UNAIDS estimates put HIV prevalence in South Africa at 18.1% of adults between the ages of 15–49 in 2007. See www.unaids.org/en/KnowledgeCentre/HIVData/GlobalReport/2008/ (accessed 1 July 2009).

FLUX OBSERVATION

The business of health and wellness

Loren Phillips

Mᴀɪɴᴛᴀɪɴɪɴɢ A healthy workforce has become an integral part of doing business in the 21st century. The recent downturn has contributed to the increasing lack of affordable healthcare with people ending up paying more and getting less in return.

A study published recently in the *American Journal of Medicine* found that 'almost two-thirds of personal bankruptcies filed in 2007 were related to medical expenses'.[1] With this in mind, it is clear that medical aids fall short of offering full coverage when it comes to chronic or life-threatening illness.[2] Furthermore, the South African government, by its own admission, cannot cope with the health needs of the entire population and is not able to offer comprehensive care for its citizens.

In South Africa, this role has been filled by the private sector, which ensures a healthy workforce (for those with medical aid schemes), in turn building a productive economy.

Both locally and abroad we are seeing a range of new businesses mushrooming to address the needs of a new breed of proactive consumers. At the same time, awareness around personal health issues is growing and people are striving to maintain optimum health to avoid the expenses and downtime related to illness. The use of alternative therapies, such as reiki and reflexology, has been on the rise for a number of years now. These are seen to offer a more holistic approach to patient care, an area where traditional Western practices may fall short.

Prevention is better than cure

South Africa is keeping pace with the globally shifting attitude of consumers towards healthcare that encourages ownership and accepts responsibility for one's own health. This is a result of the prodigious information available online and its easy accessibility. Patients can visit WebMD.com to research their symptoms and approach their general practitioners with a host of probable causes. Of course, this awareness can spiral into paranoia, a web-based hypochondria, or 'cyberchondria', but it certainly signals a broader shift towards a more proactive approach to health.

We are seeing a shift from the top down as well as from the bottom up. On the one hand, government and private companies alike are realising the financial burdens that result from caring for the sick and absenteeism due to illness, and are adopting the old maxim 'prevention is better than cure'. Although immunisation has always been a cornerstone of the national health policy, now there is a drive by local government to establish food gardens as part of the National School Nutrition Programme. This will see children in rural areas learning the value of proper nutrition and gaining the skills to harvest their own fresh produce. In the private sector, companies are establishing wellness programmes that encourage fitness and smoking cessation in order to keep their workforce healthy.[3]

On the other hand, we are also seeing individual attitudes changing with more acceptance of personal agency in one's own health and well-being. This extends across the board from exercise, healthy diet and avoiding high-risk behaviour to managing stress in a positive and beneficial manner. At the same time, people are looking beyond traditional healthcare practices to ancient arts such as yoga and t'ai chi, for the potential benefits that these have to offer. A recent study by The

George Institute for International Health showed t'ai chi to be effective in the treatment of musculoskeletal ailments such as arthritis.[4] Patients are looking beyond their doctors' rooms to explore other avenues to healing, such as the ancient Japanese art of reiki, Chinese acupuncture, *ayurvedic* medicine from India and the more modern practice of energy kinesiology, which incorporates the ancient Chinese philosophy of energy meridians into healing the body and mind.

The ancient practice of meditation has also gained a popular following in the past few years, made popular by celebrity endorsements. Filmmaker David Lynch went so far as to establish the David Lynch Foundation for consciousness-based education and world peace,[5] which teaches transcendental meditative techniques to promote healing and creativity. Today meditation is advertised on the pages of beauty and health magazines as a way of calming the mind and finding stillness in an often-chaotic world. Meditation has been proven in numerous studies to stabilise the autonomic nervous system, decrease blood pressure, encourage deep relaxation, and promote the production of serotonin – which leads to a heightened feeling of elation and happiness. Positive thinking is now being prescribed by doctors and yoga instructors alike as a tool to foster positive mental health.

Viral health

The trend of healthy living is, well, going viral. The proactive interest in managing one's own health has spurned a host of websites that enable people to take charge of their health. One of these is the California-based TheCarrot.com that offers a range of tools that assist you to track your own health and well-being. The site covers a broad range of topics, such as exercise and medicine, and other lifestyle-related issues such as sleep, TV-watching habits and job satisfaction, which all relate to well-being. There are also similar services that allow patients with Internet access to track everything from their diet to sexual health.

Aside from online start-ups, brick-and-mortar companies that offer customised wellness programmes for employees are confirming the relationship between health and productivity.

The new swing towards maintaining good health is changing business in two ways. Firstly, big corporations are adopting a more active/preventive stance in employee health. Secondly, new businesses are being founded and new products and services are popping up based solely on the idea of health.

The corporate approach

International companies such as IBM and PepsiCo have continued funnelling resources into their wellness programmes, despite the economic downturn. IBM introduced financial incentives to participate in its twelve-week fitness programme, spending more than US$133 million in 2008. A recent article in *Time* pointed out that on average, 'for every dollar that a company spends on helping employees get healthier, it can expect to save US$3 in health-care expenses'.[6]

An article in the *Journal of Occupational and Environmental Medicine* says every dollar in medical and pharmacy expenses that companies pay is dwarfed by the US$2.50 paid in health-related productivity costs.[7] 'In productivity and health-care costs combined, we've saved about US$100 million over the past three years,' says Joyce Young, IBM's Director of Wellness.[8]

At PepsiCo headquarters employees are offered pilates, spinning and yoga classes as well as free laundry services for gym clothes, all at US$20 per month.[9]

The Director of Michigan's Health Management Research Center, Dee Edington, says that keeping employees fit and productive is vitally important to a company's success, adding that the cost of an ailing worker goes beyond the financial impact of medical expenses and includes paying for leave and the strain on productivity and colleagues owing to a sick employee being non-effective at work.[10]

Virgin has echoed this thinking in the development of Virgin Life Care, which was named by Prepaid Media as the 'Most Innovative Consumer Driven Health Care Wellness Program'.[11] The programme offers people access to information and experts who can help them achieve their health and fitness goals by creating personalised eating and exercise plans and tracking their results. Locally, Virgin Life Care has partnered with Discovery and Momentum and members are rewarded with points for taking an assessment, signing a no-smoking declaration, or checking their cholesterol. People are rewarded to stay healthy, as opposed to penalised for getting sick – on the whole a healthier and more positive business model.

In an interview with Dr Craig Nossel, Head of Vitality Wellness at Discovery, he discussed 'behavioural economics' whereby people are incentivised, either financially or with other benefits, to change their behaviour. The company has created a wellness programme that targets the rise of chronic lifestyle diseases. Incentives include creating rewards for staying healthy, such as discounted movie tickets through Ster Kinekor or discounted air tickets from Kulula. Discovery has now partnered with leading supermarket chain Pick 'n Pay to offer price discounts on healthier food options. For example, a Vitality member can get a reduced price on fat-free milk or pay the full price for full cream. The 'Vitality Healthy Food' initiative offers up to 25% off on more than 6 000 Pick 'n Pay products.

In addition to incentivising healthy behaviour, it is becoming more and more important to ensure that interventions and communications are personalised; what works for a young male triathlete won't work for an elderly woman who is overweight, hypertensive, diabetic and sedentary.

Nossel also noted a rise in chronic diseases of lifestyle such as high blood pressure, raised cholesterol, obesity and diabetes, which all contribute towards increased morbidity and mortality from complications such as strokes and heart attacks. He attributes these to increasingly sedentary lifestyles where activities such as riding a bicycle or playing soccer have to compete more and more with watching TV or playing video games. The way we work as well as our leisure time is far more sedentary.

According to Nossel, healthy behaviours need to be established from a young age and implemented as a way of life, which is why Discovery has developed a schools programme that currently has more than 1 300 participating schools nationwide. The programme provides lesson plans and workshops for teachers in order to integrate health education and fun physical activities into the curriculum. In the interests of benefiting all, the lesson plans are available on the Department of Education website and these can be taught using minimal resources.[12]

Smart business moves

As a result of raised awareness of health issues, people are paying more attention to what they eat. All things organic, home-grown and local are gaining in popularity.[13] In Paris, old-school coffee shops, the hallmark of Parisian life, are being overshadowed by health bars that offer organic sandwiches and juices with a side order of a relaxing massage. 'No Stress Café' is just one example of this new breed of health-conscious cafés.

In keeping with the trend of healthy eating, Veggietrader.com is a recently launched website that allows registered users to connect with people in their area to barter fresh produce, which has a higher nutritional value than the store-bought, overpackaged variety that is picked before it is fully ripe and begins losing nutrients moments after it has been harvested.

People increasingly want to choose healthier options, which is why global companies not usually associated with health products are changing tack. For example, Pepsi UK has launched Pepsi Raw, a natural cola that uses real sugar instead of the cheaper, unhealthier substitute, corn fructose. The soda also contains apple extract, coffee leaf, tartaric acid extracted from grapes and gum arabic from acacia trees.[14] This begs the question: will unhealthy sodas survive in a health-conscious era?

Many businesses are diversifying to offer health-related products and services. Discount department store chain Walmart in the USA has recently launched 'Minute Clinic', which offers the convenience of a walk-in service.[15] In South Africa, Clicks offers customers similar on-site medical care for minor ailments at an affordable rate, without the hassle of booking and having to wait to see a GP. Retail brand Woolworths has also launched an in-store pharmacy in a similar vein.

Tech trends are following suit, with a range of medical applications available to iPhone users. Over 200 health-related applications are already available through the iTunes App Store, and the new iPhone operating system (OS3) could potentially allow real-time information to be sent to the user's medical practitioner, as it is always

Techno-ailments

Sandiso Ngubane

So you're busy typing an urgent document at work and the phone rings. Your mind is racing. It's all just busy, busy, busy. You pick up the phone, put it against your ear and balance it on your shoulder whilst you continue with that all-important document. Caution! Not only is this bad work posture, it can also lead to what has come to be known as cellphone neck.

Cellphone neck, an ailment that causes a partial spasm of neck muscles, is one of the many gadget-induced ailments that are dogging the modern world, causing concern in medical circles. Doctors, psychologists and health studies are increasingly discovering that ailments that may not necessarily be new are occurring more frequently as a result of increased gadget use in society.

Among the offenders causing agony in those who use them excessively are mobile phones, iPods and gaming consoles.

One condition that might be easy to dismiss as myth is something known as Blackberry Thumb. More properly referred to as repetitive stress injury, Blackberry Thumb commonly manifests itself in the form of a sharp sting on the palm side of the thumb. It is caused by the pressure applied when using the tiny keypads of a mobile phone, be it when texting or playing games on your gadget.

It's not only small keypads that lead to agony, though. The average keyboard on your laptop or PC has also been known to lead to an ailment called Carpal Tunnel Syndrome. The elongated periods of flexing your wrist cause inflammation and put pressure on the median nerve, leading to numbness.

The National Institute of Neurological Disorders and Strokes notes that Carpal Tunnel Syndrome is most likely to affect those who work with heavy-duty machinery than those who work on their computers for long hours every day. This, however, was a result of a 2001 study and back then gadget use wasn't as frequent as it is today, with the existence of Facebook, Twitter and the upswing in text messaging.

Gadget-caused agonies are not just dogging the communication-obsessed text message fanatics among us. Gaming enthusiasts also have reason to worry.

Palmar hidradenitis is a skin disorder caused by the strenuous hand activity of gripping

TREND SNACK

Techno-ailments *continued*

a joystick, which leads to sweaty palms and results in a nasty rash.[17] The disorder was first spotted by Swiss doctors in a twelve-year-old girl whose parents brought her to a hospital with 'intensely painful sores on the palms of her hands', as BBC online reported in early 2009. The girl apparently made a full recovery within ten days of abstaining from console gaming.[18]

Nintendo's Wii has also been receiving attention from the medical field. In some players the Wii can occasionally cause sports-injury-like pain as a result of simulating actual sports movements when playing Nintendo's *Wii Sports*. The condition has been likened to

tennis elbow and was described in one news report as 'the latest ailment to develop from the video gaming era.'[19]

As we become increasingly reliant on technology for a lot of things – work, communication, even relaxation – it is understandably easy to dismiss gadget-induced ailments as nonsense. How can we go on without these gadgets after all?

But as a PlayStation spokesperson recently told the BBC: 'As with any leisure pursuit there are possible consequences of not following common sense, health advice and guidelines.'[20]

T R E N D S N A C K

connected, allowing for up-to-the-minute prescription adjustments or medical advice. Another device on the market is Johnson & Johnson's LifeScan, which allows users to monitor their blood sugar levels in real time, through their phone.[21]

Taking healthcare into your own hands

The New York Times reports that DIY healthcare is on the increase. With rising medical costs and the huge amount of information available online, people are more likely to take healthcare into their own hands than ever before. And with the proliferation of services and products available to proactive consumers, it is becoming easier and easier.

In some cases the role of the doctor is changing from being the expert to being more of a facilitator of a process. Traditional practice is also being challenged by a variety of different models on offer. One of these is American Well, a service that replaces a traditional doctor's visit with a virtual one, made possible via a webcam and an Internet connection.[22]

The negative impact of stress weighs heavily on a corporate world that has up until now valued 'profit at any cost' over employee health. Companies are realising that it is in their best interests to promote the health and wellness of their employees as employee happiness relates positively to productivity and, hence, a company's success.

Notes

1 David U. Himmelstein, Deborah Thorne, Elizabeth Warren and Steffie Woolhandler, 'Medical Bankruptcy in the United States, 2007: Results of a National Study'. *American Journal of Medicine*, June 2009.

2 Loren Steffy, 'Insured but not Covered'. Houston Chronicle Online, 13 June 2009, www.chron.com/disp/story.mpl/business/steffy/6476972.html (accessed 20 June 2009).

3 Government Communication and Information System, 'Pocket Guide to South Africa 2008/9'. www.rdp.gov.za/resource_centre/sa_info/pocketguide/2008-09. htm (accessed 29 June 2009).

4 Amanda Hall, 'Research Proves T'ai Chi Benefits for Arthritis'. The George Institute for International Health, June 2009, www.thegeorgeinstitute.org.au/events/ latest-news/research-proves-tai-chi-benefits-for-arthritis.cfm (accessed 20 June 2009).

5 See David Lynch Foundation, www.davidlynchfoundation.org (accessed 20 June 2009).

6   Anne Fisher, 'More Companies are Paying Workers to Stay Healthy'. Time Magazine Online, 21 May 2009, www.time.com/time/business/article/0,8599,1899915,00.html (accessed 2 July 2009).

7   Fisher, 'More Companies are Paying Workers to Stay Healthy'.

8   Laura Petrecca, 'Cost-Conscious Companies Reevaluate Wellness Programs'. USA Today Online, 17 June 2009, www.usatoday.com/money/workplace/2009-06-16-wellness-programs-companies_N.htm (accessed 20 June 2009).

9   Petrecca, 'Cost-Conscious Companies Reevaluate Wellness Programs'.

10 Petrecca, 'Cost-Conscious Companies Reevaluate Wellness Programs'.

11 See Virgin Life Care, www.virginlifecare.co.za/home (accessed 29 June 2009).

12 See www.thutong.doe.gov.za (accessed 29 June 2009).

13 Josh Stone, 'Why Local Produce is Better'. Articles Base, 3 June 2007, www.articlesbase.com/health-articles/why-local-produce-is-better-158222.html (accessed 24 July 2009).

14 See www.pepsiraw.com (accessed 29 June 2009).

15 Parija Kavilanz, 'Walmart Wants your Cash and Strep Throat'. See www.money.cnn.com/2009/04/13/news/economy/healthcare_retailclinics/index.htm?section=money_topstories (accessed 24 July 2009).

16 National Institute of Neurological Disorders and Stroke, 'Carpal Tunnel Syndome Facts Sheet'. See www.ninds.nih.gov/disorders/carpal_tunnel/detail_carpal_tunnel.htm (accessed 29 June 2009).

17 Mirror.co.uk, 'Gamers at Risk from PlayStation Rash'. 25 February 2009, www.mirror.co.uk/news/top-stories/2009/02/25/gamers-at-risk-from-playstation-rash-115875-21150940/ (accessed 29 June 2009).

18 Mirror.co.uk, 'Gamers at Risk from PlayStation Rash'.

19 Reuters.com, 'If it's not Tennis Elbow, it may be "Wiiitis"'. 6 June 2007, www.reuters.com/article/technologyNews/idUSN0616721120070606 (accessed 29 June 2009).

20 BBC.co.uk, 'Game Consoles "Cause Skin Sores"'. See www.news.bbc.co.uk/1/hi/health/7907489.stm (accessed 29 June 2009).

21 Brian Dolan, 'Interview: Lifescan on iPhone 3.0'. Mobihealth News, 18 March 2009, www.mobihealthnews.com/973/interview-lifescan-on-iphone-30/ (accessed 24 July 2009).

22 See www.americanwell.com (accessed 24 July 2009).

The direction of South Africa's moral compass

Where are we headed?

Bishop Paul Verryn

Paul Verryn is the Bishop of the Central District of the Methodist Church of Southern Africa and the Superintendent of the Central Methodist Mission located in downtown Johannesburg. Over the past six years the church has become known as a place of safety and shelter for the city's dispossessed. Most recently, following a spate of xenophobic attacks on foreign nationals in South Africa, this accommodation has primarily sheltered Zimbabweans who have fled that shattered country.

Verryn is the Chairperson of the Church Unity Commission in South Africa and of the South African Council for Theological Education. He also serves as Chairperson of the Ecumenical Refugees Centre, on the national executive of the South African Council of Churches and works in close alliance with organisations such as the Legal Resources Centre, Wits Law Clinic, Médecins sans Frontières, Lawyers for Human Rights and the Human Rights Commission. All of these organisations are committed to the protection of and advocacy for human rights in Africa.

Verryn obtained a Bachelor of Arts (BA) degree from the University of South Africa in 1973 and a Bachelor of Divinity from Rhodes University in 1979. More recently, he received a Doctorate in Education *honoris causa* from the Nelson Mandela Metropolitan University.

THE EVENTS of May and June 2008 and the ongoing sporadic incidents of what we now call xenophobia revealed some profound truths to the South African community. Of course, the very term 'xenophobia' is somewhat ambivalent in that the essential emotion is not necessarily one of fear but more of anger. Not anger as 'heated' irritation or being cross, but rather an anger that seems to have its origins in history and its expression in obscene violence.

The juxtaposition of a burning man pleading for mercy and the laughing, jeering faces of the bystanders reveals a profound and disconcerting incongruence,[1] and the stories of people being disembowelled exposes more than simple demonisation.

When we consider that 61 people perished in the attacks of 2008 and that pitifully few people have been convicted in our courts for their murders, we are confronted with the abysmal performance of our policing and legal services. When we continue to be confronted by the unmitigated hate speech and gossip relating to foreign nationals and when threats of another uprising against whoever may be considered a stranger in this country continue, we sense a brooding storm on the horizon.

When the discourse of those in authority refuses to accept the considerable disintegration of the social cohesion of some of the nations north of South Africa, we realise that political expediency has become far more important than the truth. When we are forced to recognise that, in fact, very little work has been done in society to try and alert the public to the danger of further outbreaks of hate, we may be poised on the brink of much pain. If we happen to think that the atrocities will stop at foreign nationals, we had best take another look at similar movements of fascism in recent history.

Not to make too fine a point of the last sentence, but to be accurate about the figures revealed (and I must confess that these statistics have been gleaned from speeches I have heard from different people at various times), we must note that twenty South Africans were among those murdered. Only one white person was killed in the attacks, revealing that the focus was particularly on the black and poor.

In 1994 this country was catapulted from being the polecat of the globe to being the princess with the golden spoon in her mouth. Indeed, some of the achievements, not least of which was the Truth and Reconciliation Commission, were nothing short of a miracle. But for us to imagine there was no blood cost to the resolution is simply naive.

The hostel warfare, the throwing of bodies onto train tracks, the unmitigated agony of KwaZulu-Natal, the humiliation of Boipatong and the Vaal region, the violent breeding of third forces infiltrating every movement of hope, were salient warnings of our unwillingness and inflexibility in the face of change. We must remember that the formulation of a splendid Constitution – non-racist, non-ethnic, non-sexist and non-ageist – does not mean that the soul of the nation has transformed at all. In fact, in some respects, like the Bible, the Constitution simply serves as an inoculation from the truth.

We must recognise that we are a people steeped in prejudice, cultivated and watered by ignorance and an ethic perpetuated by bullying, abuse and violence. The old vestiges of bias remain by and large unaddressed, and the splendour of our diversity has been undermined by our escalating jealousies and our narrow-minded insecurities.

If the image of the rainbow captured our imaginations as a new marriage of hope, freedom and celebration, the honeymoon is over. A new image needs to be explored and far more intentional work must be done on our deep, underlying suspicions if the foundation of the future is to hold.

The disgraceful statistics of rape indicate a disease in our basic human relationships. To have to countenance budgets being spent formally and informally on policing systems and security that quite frankly are impotent and unable to address the crude criminality of our society, is indicative that these systems have no more value than make-up on an exhausted face.

One of the most severe results of apartheid expressed itself economically. Discrimination left many South Africans with poor health services, disabled educational facilities and achievements in keeping the majority of the people out of competing for economic success. The danger of the paradigm was that the boundaries set for participation were so confined that the transition in 1994 could not break open these restrictions without the country appearing as if it were turning socialist, and therefore a threat to what is perceived as financial prosperity.

Although the language used particularly around election time is suggestive of the doors of sharing being flung open to the masses, there is no doubt that those doors are so reinforced that for the majority of the poor in this country, very little hope of transition is on the horizon. Their fate is to stand at fences and barricades and watch sleek entourages making their way to obscene and expensive banqueting halls. Probably the most alarming of such displays was Robert Mugabe's birthday party on the border of Zimbabwe and South Africa in a context in which his own people were (and are) fleeing from hunger in a country with shops denuded of any provisions. People are risking their lives because of hunger, crossing a crocodile-infested Limpopo River to apparent safety.

It must be noted at this point that the South African economy has benefited handsomely from the misfortune of Zimbabwe's catastrophe but naturally, there has been very little public acknowledgement or recognition of those fiscal transactions. Firstly, if there are about 3 million Zimbabweans in this country, the contribution that they make to our economy for their mere survival benefits our retail markets handsomely. Secondly, a visit to Park Station in Johannesburg and a peep into the buses leaving for Zimbabwe daily will reveal few passengers but loads of all kinds of commodities being sent back home to refurbish houses and to feed extended families. Thirdly, the huge contribution that is made throughout this country by foreign nationals to our transport system cannot be overstated. People on the move are people who will pay whatever to reach their kingdom in the sky – their place of milk and honey. Finally, we would do well to note that it is not only China that is colonising Africa; the expansion of South African business into places of vulnerability is well established.

For many South Africans, the transition of 1994 promised a radical new beginning. Unfortunately, some factors have militated against the fair sharing of the resources of this country across the board. Corruption, greed and crime in the well-heeled sector, among white and black, have also slammed the doors shut.

It is a strange ambiguity that living in a country that is so wealthy, the poor should face such abject alienation. It is the responsibility of those who lead to ensure that appropriate systems are in place to prevent the legitimisation of crime, especially by the poor. It is important that political systems protect the right of the majority to participate in the economy of the country.

What has happened in South Africa is that by and large the trade unions, which we would imagine would be at the forefront of the struggle for the poor, have been co-opted into protecting the rights of the middle class.

The creation of job opportunities for people who have never had a place in the sun is unconvincing. We are faced with many thousands of young people who have struggled their way through an incompetent education system only to find that whatever they have managed to acquire after twelve to fifteen years of schooling is almost meaningless in the job market. There is so much to be done to improve service delivery and healthcare, so many skills needed to improve the infrastructure of this country, but somehow there exists an impasse in connecting people power to these demands. The statistic that 33% of South African households survive on a per-capita income of less than R480 a month[2] shows that we simply use those who have tried to acquire some skills as cheap, unsustainable labour, and the precariousness of their financial stability creates unmitigated anxiety for well over 40% of the nation. Sadly, political promises evaporate in the scorching heat of the lustful greed of the 'haves' in our society.

It is disgraceful that in a city such as Johannesburg whose streets are literally lined with gold and the blood of those who have succumbed to appalling mining conditions, there are still people who have slept on those streets for the past twenty years with no convincing social development programme to turn the tide and offer something different to the hopeless.

It is despicable that building after building stands guarded and empty when on freezing winter nights, people must sleep on the streets because there is no hospitable room as an alternative. It is impossible to believe, and shamefully dishonest, to claim that the nation somehow cares for the marginalised and the poor. Beyond a shadow of doubt, the promises of our liberators are comprehensively empty. And finally, their attitude is one of vicious disregard for those who may remind them of what could so easily happen to any one of us, should our tide of fortune change.

We must recognise that for most whites the transition of 1994 has delivered many more surprises of entrenching their wealth than could ever have been imagined. At the present moment the greed that is destroying this country has one success though – it knows no race.

In a society that carries such enormous religious baggage and that apparently is underpinned by a philosophy of *ubuntu* – humanity – the ever-increasing disintegration of the family is alarming to say the least. The exponential increase in child-headed households, the lowering of the life expectancy of average South Africans and the decimating instability with which poverty threatens the family unit – all these point to anarchy and despair.

We do not have systems in place that can deal with the nuanced psychological, social and emotional effects and complications of a disintegrating social fabric. To add to this agenda, the complexities of human trafficking and child abuse underscore the precarious nature of our humanity.

When children are faced with a choice as to whether they should go to school or find a menial job to support their siblings, we must realise we are tampering with the foundations of our future. When children of age fifteen have been exposed to more of life's disabilities and taken decisions which we would rarely expect a forty year old to handle, then we need to understand that an army of social workers, therapists and youth workers must be put in place to re-construct some of the damage to our society at this time. To drive children to the brink of criminal professionalism at the age of twelve and thirteen indicates that our corruption is far more invidious and pervasive than we are prepared to admit. And because we may not be exposed at this point in time to these phenomena, does not mean that we can continue to pretend they do not exist. A tide is growing.

We have not begun to understand the absolute devastation of the HIV/AIDS pandemic. In fact, most of us swan around in cloud cuckoo land still imagining that potatoes and other vegetables are all that are needed to counteract this disaster. There are very few signs that indicate an anticipation of the deluge of grief that awaits us in this regard in the next ten years. As a society we still find it awk-ward and unnecessary to talk about sex realistically and openly. We hide in the skirts of religious appropriateness and cultural niceties.

The costs of these nice feelings are exponential. Not only do we have difficulty with the discourse, but to imagine that we have any insight into a moral constraint with regard to sex generally would be absurd. If we complain that promiscuity lies at the heart of our vulnerability to the pandemic, and we then propose abstinence or fidelity as the remedy, we cannot embark on this precarious road without being very specific about sexual practice and without ex-tensive soul searching and dialogue on the realities of libido.

To imagine that we can stand in judgement as a society, and that *that* not in itself be considered immoral, is an injustice. At some level, indeed, we are an over-indulged, profane society. We have not had the wisdom to learn from the agony of our history and we have behaved as those who are callous and insensitive to the poignant pain of our brothers and sisters.

There is another angle to this compass that must be exposed in our struggle to reveal the truth. Despite the fact that the issues surrounding foreign nationals are framed in 'problem' language and in a way that can precipitate a sense of hopelessness, there is a side to this engagement that is exhilarating and bears the seeds of a future humanity emerging for this continent. Apartheid did not only separate nations and tribes in this southern tip of Africa; it inadvertently divorced this nation from its family, creating an island of supercilious arrogance and defensiveness.

At a recent community gathering words were spoken by foreign nationals to South Africans suggesting we should find a way of healing ourselves from centuries of violence and contempt. Fundamentally, that healing cannot take place in isolation.

Reconciliation is far more than hearing the truth. It involves the process of reconstructing and restoring dignity to those who in our perceptions are the enemy, whereas actually they are brothers and sisters. Rehabilitation to the point of equality, in every respect, is the secret longing of this nation.

There are voices muffled and seemingly irrelevant that must be magnified for this quest. Learning to celebrate our diversity and recognise our common humanity, the identification of our biases and the ability to transcend false idealism in this regard should be fundamental and obligatory learning in all educational institutions.

There are far more people than we can imagine who want this new beginning, not just in South Africa but in the world as a whole. For instance, fundamentally, what is the essential difference between a Jew and a Palestinian, or for that matter between a Saddam Hussein and a George Bush? For this context white racism must still be understood very carefully because it persists, but equally black racism must be addressed for its ultimate destiny will be the destruction, the complete destruction, of the hope of this nation.

It does seem as if nestled in the archive of our conscience there is a fundamental understanding that the justice of the courts remains impotent if the poor are not treated justly. At the height of the xeno-phobic violence there was clearly another dynamic operating in the minds of many South Africans. People from every conceivable walk of life, people who would be considered very rich as well as people who have very meagre resources, were determined to express their humanity in giving to alleviate the disregarded and dispossessed amongst the foreign nationals. People gave food, money, clothing, toiletries and every imaginable gift to say that this new dreadful violence did not belong to their ethos.

The appearances on the face of the country's map of informal settlements in the 1980s is nothing to compare with the escalated present multiplication of informal housing in each small village of this land. In some instances, the extent of informal settlement is eas-ily treble the size of the formal settled housing in the same area. Despite the figures relating to Reconstruction and Development Programme (RDP) housing, and despite the fact that the prevailing attitude to this spending is congratulatory, it must be said that un-fortunately this is too little too late.

We need to remember that from 1976 to at least 1990, the then government spent almost nothing on housing for the marginalised. This means that if there is to be restitution, it implies huge expend-iture and this should be long before cities which have reasonable in-frastructure gentrify even further the avenues of the rich. This funda-mental imbalance simply must be set straight. We have more than fourteen years of neglect that must be reconciled before we spend any further money on any other parts of the budget that simply protect the rights of the rich and ignore the grinding struggle of the poor.

We may not understand fully the unleashed crime on our streets, but we need to recognise that this is a gentle beginning of a far more profound revolution, which history teaches us will ultimately not consider high walls, electric fences or burglar alarms. The present disparity between the rich and the poor is a perfect recipe for an unbridled revolution.

There are many in this country in all strata of society who know this fact instinctively and who want an alternative for our people. When we faced the monolithic, impenetrable designs of apartheid, we could never have imagined anything different than a bloody revolution. But the walls crumbled almost unbelievably overnight.

The same reality can be applied to this impasse. The tide in the right direction is waiting to be unleashed for a new humanity. The walls seem as impenetrable as were the walls of apartheid. They must crumble as comprehensively. That moral hope is there. The seeds of hope are in the minds of those who are alive and express their impatience in protest and in demonstration just as in our past. Somehow, in listening to hope articulated in anger, the seed may possibly be given the space to germinate.

Finally, it seems as if our intimate relationships reflect something of the chaos of our economic integrity. There is a re-alignment happening in the power relations between men and women and all other spheres of interaction. A new design for our interactions is emerging and is re-defining itself. Words like dignity, humanity, respect, fidelity and grace, are shaping a new future.

The interface between our very real hopelessness and our very vulnerable imagination is fragile. The choices we make for our future are very much like the choices between life and death. And strangely, if not ironically, the popular choices imply death. The time has passed for populist and manipulative speculation. Our leadership must be seen to make the unpopular moral call for the sake of the survival of this continent. We must be prepared to recognise that some of the leadership exists not in the loud and garish voices of the dominant but in the silenced majority who may come to meetings and say nothing, but who in actual fact carry the solution to this intricate and complex conundrum. A process must be defined that will insist on hearing the silenced and on redefining our fundamental understanding of democracy.

Notes

1 The man being referred to is Ernesto Alfabeto Nhamuave, a 35-year-old Mozambican national who was burned alive on the streets of Ramaphosa settlement, on Gauteng's East Rand, during a wave of xenophobic attacks in May 2008.

2 'The Bottom of the Pyramid', Eighty20 Study, 2009, see www.eighty20.co.za (accessed 28 June 2009).

Conclusion

Breaking the mould

Dion Chang

IT IS said that throughout our lifetimes we all encounter a number of peak experiences that construct as well as alter our perspectives on life. These peak experiences range from emotionally draining episodes, such as the death of a loved one, to small, seemingly insignificant ones that stick in our minds, such as childhood memories of tastes and smells. These memories come together like a giant jigsaw puzzle and paint a picture we all call reality. Sometimes we experience things not as individuals but as a collective. Take 9/11, for example. As the planet witnessed the twin towers collapse, we all instinctively knew that the world had changed forever.

Nobody had to say it; we just knew.

In much the same way – although not instantaneously – the world is currently undergoing a universal peak experience. It may have been sparked off by the global economic meltdown but that is proving to be only the tip of a very large and significant peak experience. It may feel as if all we need to do is weather the financial storm, but the dark clouds of change that converged for this perfect storm were gathering force way before the financial markets tumbled.

Seemingly disparate movements, such as the rise of civil society, the eco movement, the evolution of social networks, conspicuous consumption and even – in its own vacuous way – the cult of the celebrity, have all altered the mood of society enough to create a monumental tipping point that the global recession set in motion.

Just as we all instinctively knew that 9/11 had changed the world, so too are we all beginning to understand that once the financial crisis stabilises, it would be foolhardy to think that life will continue the way it did eighteen months ago. Value systems have shifted significantly, and those value systems are overarching, whether they are our attitude to extravagant spending habits, the environment or the politicians we elect.

We have been travelling in the fast lane on the information highway for far too long. Now it's time to take a detour and switch to a quieter, less frenetic route, one that provides ample opportunity to stop, refocus our thoughts and reassess the journey ahead.

Getting in touch with your feminine side

In the trend world, much has been written about the coming of the female century. I need to point out that this has nothing to do with a postmodern feminist movement, but more to do with a balancing of aggressive or bullish behaviour that has dominated the business and political arenas for so long. Many believe that it was this very same, profit-at-all-cost attitude that got us into this financial mess in the first place – and clearly, it is unsustainable.

But it is not only about codes of conduct in business and politics. The very real prospect of killing the environment that sustains us, and in the process self-destructing as a species, has seeped into global consciousness, specifically among the younger generation that will have to deal with the consequences. This heightened awareness, or mindfulness, has started a chain reaction that, with the help of technology, is shifting mindsets around the globe.

Michelle Obama is the embodiment of this new mindset. *Time* magazine explained this succinctly when it commented: 'She arrives at a place where her power is amplified by her apparent lack of interest in it.'[1] It reported that when the Obama family moved into the White House Michelle called a meeting with her existing communications and policy staff from Chicago and her new White House staff. She told her existing staff that her new (predominantly household) staff would not be judged by whether or not they knew the names of the advisory staff, but rather that her advisory staff would be judged if they did not know the names of the domestic staff. It was a subtle but seminal shift in attitude, ego and priority ... and it speaks volumes about how our brave new world could, and should, operate.

The empathetic economy

So what is the significance of connecting to your feminine side? Empathy.

The global recession has heightened the awareness of others less fortunate in society. When companies retrenched their staff, the pain was felt by both management and co-workers who retained their jobs. The culling of the global workforce will have far-reaching consequences as we move into 2010 and beyond. It will force many to reassess their careers, what they do (or have always wanted to do), what really brings fulfilment, and whether it is worth sacrificing one's health or time, which could have been better spent with loved ones, for financial reward.

With the help of technology, the recession will see a boom in innovation and entrepreneurship. Small start-up companies that offer personalised services, bespoke products and flexible management will step into the widening change gap that larger companies are failing to narrow.

With tools like social networks at their disposal, and empowered by 'armchair wisdom' (courtesy of the Internet), today's consumers are proving to be tough to please, or even speak to. Thanks to the recession, they are highly distrusting of large, monolithic corporations that don't recognise the individual.

Smaller companies will be better equipped to engage on a personal level with their customers, as well as to accommodate vastly different needs. For the larger companies, it will become increasingly important to show empathy if they are to regain consumer trust and appeal.

Already the trend for social corporate investment has become widespread, but this will accelerate. It will become less of a point of differentiation, and more of a basic policy that all consumers will expect, influencing consumers' brand loyalty to companies. Corporate social investment cannot be an activity that is used as a marketing tool. It is an ethos that has to filter through the company's structures. The relationships between employer and worker, service provider and consumer are set to change dramatically in the next couple of years.

Complex journeys, simple routes

The empathetic economy, or enhanced feminine values, will also have a long-term impact on design and design cycles. We have been running on a treadmill of disposable design for far too long, whether it is fast fashion, throwaway home decor or techno gadgetry (each year in America alone there are 500 million obsolete computers and 130 million mobile phones thrown away).[2]

The global recession has made us more aware of our wasteful

habits and, backed by increased awareness for our environment, has instilled in us the mantra of reduce, reuse, recycle. Against this backdrop, consumers have started reviewing their purchases. Evidence is already emerging that consumer habits are changing; instead of buying cheap and disposable items often, consumers are buying better-quality items less frequently. This 'flight to quality' was noted in the Flux observation, 'Redeeming the reputation of luxury'. As well as this migration to a higher standard of quality, there is also a parallel trend towards product design becoming simpler, with the focus on functionality rather than gadgetry.

In Korea, one of the world's key manufacturers of appliances, this trend is already unfolding, and again, the change of strategy has been sparked by the economic downturn. In order to introduce more affordable items into a depressed market, manufacturers have cut non-essential gadgetry from their products and instead are producing more practical items that are nevertheless still beautifully designed. This shift has been hugely successful, indicating that consumers are more than ready to simplify their lives and embrace functionality rather than frivolity.

In many ways this yearning to simplify our lives illustrates a willingness to reassess our value systems. People are going back to basics (and loving it), while companies are reviewing their core strengths or functions and refocusing their energies rather than dissipating them. Keeping it simple and real seems to be the philosophy that works for these troubled times. People are searching for authenticity on every level, whether in an election promise from a politician or in a TV advert for a product or service. In this quest for authenticity, people have started to turn to trusted sources – friends, family or communities – for advice, which is why the concept of tribes becomes so important.

Touch, pause, engage

As more 21st-century tribes begin to form, changes in social dynamics will become faster and more dramatic. The world is beginning to resemble a giant schoolyard with different groups of friends forming on the basis of their shared interests or even shared rejection of mainstream society.

As these gangs of nerds, jocks, academics, creative misfits, rebels and the like huddle in their respective corners, they begin creating new rules or codes of conduct for their members, and the voices of authority find it increasingly difficult to breach their inner sanctum or decipher their coded communication.

In essence, this is what is happening across the planet as we head into the second decade of the 21st century. The restructuring of social groups who are techno-savvy and have global connectivity (with real-time interaction) is causing a seismic shift in thinking and forcing us all to re-map the journey ahead. All the rules we have played by until now have changed, but we are left with few clues as to what the new guidelines are or should be. For many, navigating this uncertain path is terrifying, while some find it invigorating.

At Flux, we see the wheels of change turning quite visibly, and the need to adapt to this change is unequivocal. We see it in the companies we consult for and in the trend research we delve into. The common thread that is emerging is a gradual acknowledgement that certain modes of conduct and many long-established methodologies are fast becoming outdated, ineffectual or redundant. In some industries the trend indicators point to revisiting the past: for example, the old, tried-and-tested concept of word-of-mouth marketing is proving to be surprisingly successful for the advertising industry where mass marketing is failing. In other industries completely new concepts are being test-driven, such as creating full-time positions for social network managers to handle a company's online profile. But the goalposts have shifted overall and boundaries have blurred.

Today, adverts need to be classified as 'branded entertainment' if there is any hope of attracting anyone's attention. And in most cases, the product being advertised is not the focus; rather, it is the lifestyle context in which the product sits that is the focus. The current measure of success of any advert's worth is whether or not it has been spread virally on YouTube – or on social networks – by the tribe it was destined for. Even then, thanks to innovations like the PVR, many have started rejecting scheduled programming, preferring to design their own entertainment schedules rather than to fit their busy schedules into a broadcaster's timetable. New rules indeed.

Engaging with change at this juncture is crucial. While the rulebook is being rewritten, opportunities abound for those who are prepared to look at society from a fresh perspective and are willing to blaze new trails.

If 2009 was the year we all licked our wounds, 2010 will be the year in which we regroup, reassess and move forward. At Flux we anticipate that the change we are experiencing now will gain momentum and acceptance, and accelerate between 2010 and 2012. Ask yourself now: would you prefer to be riding that wave of change or be trapped swimming against the tide?

Notes

1 Nancy Gibbs and Michael Scherer, 'Michelle Up Close'. *Time*, 1 June 2009.
2 Patrick Dixon, 'Hazards from 500 Million Old Computers'. Globalchange.com, www.globalchange.com/how-green-is-your-it-digital-world.htm (accessed 24 July 2009).